Your Holiday Feast

Cookbook & Planning Guide

Kay Rice, M.Ed.

Copyright © 2015 by Kay Rice

No part of this publication may be reproduced or transmitted in any form or by any means, mechanical or electronic, including photocopying and recording, or by any information storage and retrieval system, without permission in writing from author or publisher (except by a reviewer, who may quote brief passages and/or show brief video clips in review)

ISBN-13:
978-0615908847 (Spontaneous Health, LLC)

ISBN-10:
0615908845

Published by:

Spontaneous Health, LLC

Cover Design by:

Maryann Brown

www.creativemarketingcafe.com

Dedication

Your Holiday Feast is dedicated to Mike Rice and our children,

Sabra, Jake & Tanner Rice,

Our extended Rice Family,

And to our future family members and additions.

Table of Contents

Dedication	Iii
Preface	Ix
Introduction	xi
Organization & Planning	1
Appetizers & Snacks	19
Holiday Party Mix	20
Dill Crab Dip	21
Mexican Pinwheels	22
Spicy Tomato Cheddar Spread	23
Hot & Spicy Chicken Dip	24
Cream Cheese with Sweet Pecan Topping	25
Beverages	31
Citrus Punch	32
Chocolate Martinis	33
Shenandoah Road Eggnog	34
Breads & Muffins	39
Banana Bread	40
Breakfast Muffins	41
Cranberry-Orange Nut Bread	42
Pumpkin Bread	43
Breakfast Casseroles	49
Apple Cranberry Breakfast Pudding	50
Breakfast Casserole	51
Cheese Grits Casserole	52
Jay's Omelet Casserole	53
Eggs Benedict Casserole	54

Cakes   *59*

Apple Cake	60
Apple Sheet Cake	61
1-2-3-4 Basic Yellow Cake	62
Pineapple Upside Down Cake	63
Caramel Icing	64
Tidewater Chocolate Pound Cake	65
Fluffy Cocoa Frosting	66
Favorite Carrot Cake	67
Cream Cheese Frosting	68
Mima's Strawberry Short Cake	69
Sweet Potato, Chocolate Pecan Cake	70
White Chocolate Raspberry Cheese Cake	71

Candies & Cookies   *79*

Chocolate Fudge Candy	80
M&M Holiday Cookies	82
Mexican Chocolate Cherry Rounds	83
No-Bake Cookies	84
Peanut Butter Cookies	85
Teacakes	86

Pastries & Pies   *93*

Whole Wheat Pie Crust	95
Apple Pie	96
Cran-Apple Pie	97
Blackberry Pie	98
Cherry Pie	99
Chocolate Mint Pie	100
Custard Pie	101
Pecan Pie Squares	102
Classic Pumpkin Pie	103
Orange Sweet Potato Pie	104
Orange Crust	105

Holiday Entrees   *111*

Preparing a Turkey	112
Chicken Broth	118
Make-Ahead Turkey Gravy	119
Cranberry Sauce	120

Essential Bread Dressing	121
Roasted Turkey	122
Deep Fried Turkey	125
Beef Prim Rob Roast Cooking Tips	127
Beef Prime Rib Roast with Roast Potatoes	128
Easy Beef Prime Rib Roast	130
Slow Cooked Pork Roast with Sauerkraut	131

Vegetable Side Dishes — 137

Basic Mashed Potatoes	138
Butterbeans with Bacon	139
Corn Casserole	140
Green Bean Casserole	141
Southern Squash Casserole	142
Sweet Potato Casserole	143
New Year Pot of Greens	144
Roasted Brussel Sprouts	145

Turkey Leftovers & Miscellaneous — 151

War Eagle Barbeque Sauce	152
Boiled Peanuts	153
Chicken Enchiladas	154
Rifrito Casserole	155
Turkey Tetrazzini	156
Alfredo Sauce	157
Hot Brown Sandwiches	158

Appendix A: Look Who's Coming — 165

Appendix B: Holiday List & Time Table — 167

Appendix C: Meal Schedule — 173

Appendix D: Pre-Holiday Shopping List — 175

Appendix E: Holiday Shopping List — 177

Appendix F: Memories & Tradition — 179

Appendix G: Holiday Games — 184

Preface

This book was written for everyone who will host a holiday dinner or family reunion. If you have never baked a turkey, made gravy, or cooked for such a large crowd, this guide is for you. If you find the planning and preparation for a large family meal or hosting and welcoming a large group for several days an overwhelming task, this book will help you. If you want some tips on how to make every one of your guests feel welcome and at home, I think you will find some useful suggestions.

There is an art to making your home welcoming to others who have traveled from across the country or from the other side of the world. They have different food preferences, different time schedules, different habits, and they may have forgotten some all-important item when they arrive. A good hostess makes them feel comfortable and at home with what seems like effortless ease. It takes some planning, and the right attitude, but it is really quite simple. I'll tell you what works for my family and for me.

Some families dread the holidays. All too often the holidays are associated with unpleasant family issues and stress. That has not been our experience; we learned years ago not to sweat or stress over the small stuff. We look forward to our holiday gatherings months in advance. The planning and preparation is fun! It has been a big part of my children's experience, and has given them some of their fondest memories. I look forward to my children and their cousins carrying this tradition forward, and I am confident they will.

The recipes in this book are tried and true; I've included all of our family favorites! Some of these recipes have come from generations ago. Please use them, and add your own family favorites to them. At the end of each chapter I have included a few additional pages for you to add your own favorite recipes, notes, or to include anything else you choose. I like to "stick to the favorites" and then experiment with a new recipe or two each year. Some are hits and get added to the annual menu—others have bombed. I have learned there are certain recipes I do not experiment with. I can remember one particular holiday when I tried a "variation" on the type of bread I used in our turkey dressing. The day after the event my sister-in-law came into the kitchen and very diplomatically addressed me, "Kay, can we talk about the dressing?" I already knew I'd made a mistake. That is one of the recipes I should never experiment with.

Introduction

Hosting a Holiday Feast or Family Reunion is a GIFT! You are not just preparing food; you are creating an experience and an atmosphere for traditions, memories, and connection between friends and family. These experiences will last for a lifetime and possibly will be carried on to future generations. It isn't just about the food and the menu, but the experiences we have at these events. Eventually, the traditional foods and recipes will trigger the memory of the experience of these events and gatherings.

The first time I hosted a family holiday gathering and cooked for a large family it seemed like an overwhelming task. I was fairly new to the family, pregnant with my first child, and of course I wanted everything to be perfect and to impress my husband's extended family.

The planning and preparation of a Holiday Meal was something I'd never done. I'd never cooked a turkey, made dressing or gravy, or entertained that many people at once, especially over several days. I didn't have enough chairs, or dishes, or silverware! I felt the pressure of wanting everything to turn out perfectly! Trust me, things are never PERFECT, and how you handle the unexpected is a key piece of putting on a successful event. There is a way to use what you have, not break the bank, and still have a great event and make everyone feel welcome and at home. I'll show you how.

I don't remember any particular thing going terribly wrong at that first holiday reunion, but I do remember I felt a lot of stress. I learned a LOT! As the years progressed and this became an annual event I began to collect lists and recipes. I recorded the things that worked and those that didn't. I made shopping, planning and to-do lists that I could use each year. All of this made the task simpler. Although our event kept growing, it became easier to organize. I made and printed out my first "Holiday Reunion Planner" in 1998 and I gave out copies to our family members. By this time I had most of the process down to a science and I wanted to share it with everyone in the family who might benefit. My mission, just in case I ever stopped doing these reunions, was make certain that everyone else in the family had our recipes and that no one else would ever feel the overwhelm and stress I did when I began putting on this annual event.

When I presented the first edition of this Holiday Reunion Planner to our family members it was suggested that I publish it. Now, 15 years later, here it is! The first edition fit in a ½" binder. The Second Edition which I put together in 2001 needed a 2.5" Binder. I hope you will enjoy this published Edition.

Chapter 1

Organization & Planning

Kay's Blessing at Thanksgiving

A mother invited some people to dinner.

At the table she turned to her 6 year-old daughter and said, "Would you like to say the blessing?"

"I wouldn't know what to say," the little girl replied.

"Just say what you hear Mommy say," the mother answered.

The daughter bowed her head and said, "Lord, why on earth did I invite all these people to dinner?"

This Blessing was sent to me by one of my sister's-in- law one Thanksgiving holiday quite a few years ago. All kidding aside—

It has been my blessing to have planned and prepared a Holiday Family Reunion and Feast for more than two decades. This gathering, these traditions, and the recipes have been part of my children's growing up experience and are among their most cherished memories. The little children who grew up with this tradition are now grown. Many of them are now married and have children of their own. We have welcomed new *family members, babies have been born and we have lost a few members through the years. Truly, hosting this event is a labor of love. I can't tell you how gratifying it is to contribute to a family in such a way. Because we do our large gathering at Thanksgiving, all three of my children grew up with it as being their favorite holiday and the one they remember as the most fun.*

Holiday Celebrations

As family and friends consider when and where to gather during the holidays, Thanksgiving heralds the season. Our family chooses to have a Thanksgiving Reunion Celebration each year with the extended family gathering for the event from all parts of the United States and occasionally even from other countries! It has become the one event of the year that around which everyone plans their vacation schedules and travel arrangements. Since people come from other states and may drive many to get here, our Thanksgiving Celebration is much more of a reunion and event than just the Thanksgiving Day Meal. Typically, our guests begin to arrive as early as Monday and stay until Saturday morning. It takes a lot of planning and preparation to comfortably accommodate as many as 20 additional people and make them all feel welcome and at home. Each year my children enjoy the anticipation of the event as they watch the preparations begin. They enjoy watching food being prepared in advance and then stored away for our "Big Event". Our Thanksgiving Reunions created the most memorable experiences for our children. When they were in grammar school, it was always Thanksgiving rather than Christmas that they wrote about when they were asked to write about their favorite holiday.

We gather our extended family at Thanksgiving for several reasons. We have grown to be a pretty large group, and family members are scattered all across the country. This means that when they arrive they stay for several days. We decided that if we gather our extended family for Thanksgiving we didn't have to worry about whether to bring gifts for everyone, nor did we have to pack away or hide gifts as we would for Christmas. In our family this works. We keep the Christmas Holiday Celebration for our smaller family gatherings. Our annual Thanksgiving Celebration & Reunion was about family, fun, and of course the food! Cousins who lived far away from each other have grown up knowing each other and bonded because of this annual event. We've had this annual event for long enough that nieces and nephews, who were just children when we started gathering, have grown up, gotten married and now have children of their own who come to the annual event.

As the hostess, I made an executive decision regarding decorations for Thanksgiving. Rather than decorate the house for the beginning of the Christmas season, I have always chosen to keep Thanksgiving separate from the December festivities. I decorate with the house with fall colors and set the table in keeping with the Thanksgiving Tradition. The Saturday or Sunday after Thanksgiving we all put away the fall decorations, go purchase our Christmas tree fresh off the lot, and bring out our decorations for our December festivities.

Hint: If you are going to have a holiday tree, purchase it as soon as it arrives on the lot. Even if you are not ready to set it up and decorate it you can keep it fresh and its branches moist & watered by making sure its feet stay wet. Make certain the bottom of the trunk is freshly cut so it will absorb water. Set it in a large bucket or tub of water until you are ready to bring it indoors to set up and decorate it. Once it is inside be sure you continue to water it every day.

Planning & Organization

The key to making a large gathering seem effortless and easy is in the planning and the organization of the event. As the host or hostess, knowing you already have much of the work done before you first guests arrive will minimize your stress and make the event more fun for you. It is important to know that you set the tone for your guests. If you are overwhelmed, uptight and stressed about the event your guests will feel it. Conversely, a relaxed host/hostess conveys that energy and atmosphere to his/her guests, creating a welcoming and relaxed environment. In addition, how you handle the unexpected makes a difference. It helps to know in advance that no matter how well prepared and organized you are, something unexpected can, and likely will, occur. Be flexible and accept these things with grace. It is all a part of the event and how you handle these things really does make a difference.

Look Who's Coming

Start with letting your extended family and friends know months in advance that you plan to host this event. In our case, it is a standing annual event and everyone knows a year in advance and can plan accordingly. Even so, about 2 to 3 months before the event, it is good to begin making a list of who is coming, how many, when they will be arriving and how long they plan to stay. This is a great time to start thinking about where to put all of these people, too. I call this "counting heads and counting beds". I make a list each year called "Look Who's Coming." Keep the list as a memory of who was there that year. You will find copy of that list than you can use at the back of this book

Once you have a list of who is coming and when they will be arriving you can begin planning menus. It is very helpful not only to plan but to shop and prepare ahead of time as much as possible. If you have guests who would like to bring items, make a note of what they are bringing. One of our relatives sends a check each year to help with expenses. Another likes to purchase a ham for the event. Allowing your guests to contribute will not only lighten your load, but it will make them feel more a part of the celebration. Again, I prepare as much ahead of time as possible. There is an example of the chart I use for menu planning at the back of this book in Appendix C.

It helps to begin your pre-holiday preparations anywhere for three to six weeks in advance. Many recipes can be made ahead of time and stored or frozen. I always make pie crusts, fresh chicken broth and turkey gravy weeks and advance and store them in the freezer. They stay perfectly fresh when frozen for a few weeks. Loaf breads and some cakes can be made ahead of time and frozen, too.

Before you begin your holiday shopping and cooking is the perfect time to clean out and organize your pantry and freezer. You will need the space. Check your spice cabinet, supply of dry goods and staples you know you will need. Even though we don't think of spices as having an expiration date you may want to replace any that have been around for more than a year or two with fresh spices. They do lose their aroma and flavor over time and you want all of your ingredients to be the freshest and tastiest possible.

A bonus to having an annual reunion is that any projects or renovations—and we always seem to be doing something at our house—always get finished before our guests arrive. It is a great incentive to have these projects finished by a specific deadline each year.

Recipes that I make ahead of time each year include pie crusts, cake layers, cookie dough, chicken broth and turkey gravy. All of those can be made up to eight weeks in advance and frozen. You can use the chicken meat from making your broth to make Chicken Enchilada Casserole, which freezes nicely, and can be used as a main dish while you have guests. Turkey meat left over from the Make Ahead Turkey Gravy can be used in a turkey pot pie or other recipes. Bear in mind that the extra meat from these recipes you are making in advance can also be used for your family dinner on the evening you are cooking them. I can't tell you how many times my children came home to the delicious aroma of food cooking, only to find I'd spent the day cooking for Thanksgiving and had all but forgotten to plan dinner for that evening. After a few years, I learned to work it into the plan in a way that eased the load and ensures that my family has dinner, even on days when I've been doing a lot of pre-holiday cooking. For example, when I cook Chicken for the broth, I make not just one, but two, Chicken Enchilada Casseroles. One for that evening for our family, and another to go in the freezer for entertaining later.

Holiday Chex Mix and Chocolate Fudge Candy can also made at least a couple of weeks in advance. Seal them up tightly and hide them away to keep them fresh, and so they won't be eaten before your guests arrive. Every year my children and their friends eagerly await my making a big batch of Holiday Chex Mix. As much as I make, if I don't hide it, it will be completely gone by Thanksgiving. Part of the fun is making everyone in the household wait until the first guests arrive before we start eating any of the snacks and desserts prepared in advance for the event.

You will find a shopping list for Non-perishable Items & Make Ahead Recipes in Appendix D. There is a list for perishable items in Appendix E. Each year I use a timeline and several shopping lists for everything I need. I have included an example of my "Holiday Preparation List & Time Table" at the back of this book in Appendix B.

There will be so many desserts and snacks, you may find it helpful to designate a large table out of the way of kitchen traffic. Having a dessert table set up in your dining room or foyer makes a delightful and welcoming display. All of our cakes, pies, cookies, snacks and candies are placed there along with plates, forks and napkins so guests can help themselves at will. The kids have made a game of Sneak-A-Snack for years—they believed they were secretly snitching snacks off of this table when the grown-ups were not looking. Little did they know that we were all okay with their eating whatever they want. We always set aside our usual concerns about what they should eat and spoiling their appetites for meals during these few days.

Our family is full of fun and has played games and pulled pranks on one another for years. You'll find some examples of our Holiday Games in Appendix G. Of greatest importance—keep things fun. Don't ever do anything that creates a big mess for your host or hostess to clean up—and remember it is for fun. Whenever someone at our house says, "Wouldn't it be funny if—?" The response is, "Well it ain't funny unless you really do it!"

I've included some of my own notes about some of our family's Memories & Traditions in Appendix F. These have not been modified and came right from my personal notes. I suggest you used some of the pages I've included in this book for recording your family recipes that you would like to add, and to include your own memories and traditions important to your family.

Finally, it is important to make your home welcoming to out of town guests who may have different habits and preferences than yours. There are some simple things that can be done to make your guests feel comfortable serving and taking care of themselves. This makes things easier on everyone all around, and creates a more relaxed atmosphere, and makes everyone feel more "at home".

Make Your Guests Feel At Home

Discuss needs & preferences they may have before they arrive.

Find out what day and time they expect to arrive & depart. Discuss what sleeping accommodations might work best for them. If they have children, consider the ages and whether they might share the room with their parents or sleep in another space in the house. Generally, we let "the kids" sleep on couches and or in sleeping bags in the basement or family room. Bearing this in mind, be mindful that teenagers like to sleep later and make certain you choose an area away from the early morning noise and bustle in the kitchen and the chatter of early risers.

Prepare the Bedrooms

At times when our house is at maximum capacity, my children give up their bedrooms and sleep elsewhere. I have them "pack a bag" just like they were going away for a few days and bring it to the Master Bedroom/Bath so they can have access to their belongings without disturbing guests sleeping in their bedroom. The children never minded doing this; to them it was fun. Frequently, I have them sleep elsewhere the night before the guests arrive so I have an extra day to make sure the room has been thoroughly cleaned, has fresh linens, and if appropriate and available I fresh flowers or some special treat.

Prepare the Bathrooms

Have a bowl or basket available with items that your guests might need, or in case they forgot an essential item. Include items such as toothbrushes, toothpaste, mouthwash, dental floss, deodorant, shampoo, conditioner, razors and lotion. Optional items may include acetaminophen, Tylenol, adhesive bandages, cotton balls and cotton swabs. Arrange these items attractively in a bowl or basket in clear sight. This way your guests won't even need to ask if they need something. Your thoughtfulness will be noticed and appreciated even if they don't need anything. Place clean towels and washcloths where they are easily seen or found, and leave the towel bars empty so each guest can find their own spot for their towel and washcloth, re-using them during their stay. A nice touch is to add flowers or a plant, a special seasonal scented soap and hand towels.

Prepare the kitchen

Designate an area in your kitchen as the coffee/tea bar. Have coffee filters, coffee beans or grounds, mugs, sugar, sweeteners in plain sight so that if an early morning riser gets up and wants their brew they can easily start the first pot for the day. Realizing there will be a steady stream of traffic wandering through the kitchen, I keep this in mind when I decide where to set up the coffee bar so the traffic does not interfere with other kitchen and cooking activity. This will make things easier on both the hosts and the guests.

If someone has an infant or toddler with special food needs, keep in mind they may bring special foods items, dishes and appliances. Give them a space on a shelf or in the pantry to store what is needed.

Let Everyone Pitch In

One of the very best ways to make your guests feel at home and at ease in your house is to let them contribute in some way. Your guests will likely offer to help. Accept their offers and be flexible. If you are cooking and serving for several days, every little bit helps and allowing everyone the option of contributing in their own unique way allows your guests to feel more a part of the celebration. Over the years, family members may even find something they enjoy doing so much that they will take ownership of that responsibility. I can think of many examples of this, and right now I think it would be fun to make a list.

One of our family members enjoyed contributing by sending me a check a few weeks before the event. This was easy for him, and very helpful for me. Hosting a large group for several days can be costly. Each year I used a portion of his gift to purchase an item to add to my kitchen or table accessories and the remainder went toward the large grocery bill for the event.

One of the first couples to arrive often took my husband and I out for dinner at a nice restaurant on the evening of their arrival. One of their teenage sons would babysat our children when they were young. This was a wonderful way for them to treat the host & hostess and their teenager received lots of accolades for his contribution as the babysitter. The kids enjoyed having pizza ordered in and a movie and were thoroughly happy and entertained for the evening.

One of my nieces, a chef, always sharpens the knives when she arrives. Then in one sitting chops up enough onions and celery for all of the recipes we will be making during the week. Once chopped, they store nicely in zip lock freezer bags.

A nephew makes the mashed potatoes. The rest of the family is convinced that no one's mashed potatoes equal his. Here are a few family tricks he uses: Use a ricer to mash the potatoes before they are beaten. He often has help peeling the potatoes so I keep an extra potato peeler on hand. In general, allow at least one large potato per person. Purchase the large potatoes in bulk rather than in a bag. The larger ones are faster to peel and cut up. We use a very large stock pot to boil that many potatoes. Believe it or not, the mashed potatoes can be made a day in advance. Refrigerate them over-night and then in the morning warm them in the microwave, and then move them to a crock pot to keep warm, or just warm them in the crock-pot and skip the microwave process. The potatoes will need to be stirred several times during the re-heating process.

Another family member always carves the turkey for us. Our gatherings have gotten large enough that we have two turkeys, or at least one turkey and a turkey breast.

Others may want to contribute by cooking a new or favorite recipe, or bringing something to add to the dessert table.

One out-of-town relative frequently chooses to purchase a large Honey Baked Ham for the week, and would have it ready for pick up a day or two before the event. The ham is great for Ham Bone Soup, Sandwiches and of course, one of our family favorites, Jay's Omelet Casserole.

Nieces and or cousins help with table setting the morning of our big dinner.

Traditional Holiday Menus

Over the years we have tried different recipes for holiday side dishes, various recipes and methods for cooking the Holiday Turkey, and even a few times I have tinkered with the basic recipes for the dressing and mashed potatoes. I'll never forget my sister-in-law beating a huge batch of mashed potatoes in a five gallon paint bucket using a paint mixer one of the first years we gathered a large group. Later, I was able to afford a commercial sized stainless steel mixing bowl, a ricer, and an appropriate mixer for the job. If you don't know what a ricer is, until I joined this family neither did I. If you put your cooked potatoes through a ricer before whipping them it will ensure the smoothest lightest mashed potatoes you've ever eaten! You can purchase a ricer at Williams Sonoma or any high end specialty cooking store. While it is fun to experiment with an additional side dish or salad from one year to another, I learned that is was best not to deviate from what our family considered to be their traditional Family Holiday Menu. These menu items were central to the Family Feast and what the feast meant to our family members. Following are the items that our family can be certain will be on our Thanksgiving Menu every year.

Thanksgiving Menu

Turkey ~ Roasted or Fried

Dressing

Mashed Potatoes

Gravy

Homemade Cranberry Sauce

Traditional Green Bean Casserole

Corn Casserole

Sweet Potato Casserole

Pumpkin Pie & Custard Pie

Occasionally we might add a salad, or try other side dishes. You will find some of these additional recipes in Your Holiday Feast Cookbook & Planning Guide. Sometimes we have butterbeans, squash casserole, or roasted vegetables. Of course the Dessert Table is always filled with pies, cakes, cookies and homemade fudge. Other recipes may come and go but the ones listed on the menu are set in stone. I learned early on that to try to tinker with, or make these recipes fancier or deviate from the original in any way was going to result in someone being unhappy or disappointed that their favorite item was missing or didn't taste right. Rather than being boring, repetition is what makes the Traditional Holiday Menu a delicious Family Tradition!

I like to make the menu different for each celebration: Thanksgiving, Christmas and then for the New Year. Our family made a choice many years ago to gather as an extended family at Thanksgiving. We did this for a number of reasons. Most of the family had to travel, so that made having Christmas together with small children a challenge. We also decided that there were way too many nieces, nephews, cousins, etc. to make gift-giving practical at Christmas. Therefore, we made our tradition to gather as a large family, reunion style, at Thanksgiving. Our gift to each other was of being together and sharing memories, time together and great food.

We decorate the house differently for each holiday. At Thanksgiving the house and table are decorated in traditional Thanksgiving colors with turkeys, gourds, pumpkins, and fall colors. The weekend following Thanksgiving, the Thanksgiving decorations get put away and the Christmas decorations come out.

We get our tree as soon as it is available. This is generally the weekend after Thanksgiving. Some of our family purchases their tree the weekend before Thanksgiving and leaves it in a bucket of water while they are away visiting us. You may as well get your tree right away instead of letting it sit on the tree lot drying out. If you get it right away you can make certain it stays watered and fresh. A Christmas tree is the largest live plant arrangement you will ever have, so it pays to keep it fresh, watered, and enjoy its fragrance and beauty as much as possible.

One of my favorite traditions is to have all the Christmas decorations down before New Year's Day. Actually, this more than a tradition, it is a superstition that has been passed down to me. I grew up being told that it was "bad luck" if you still have Christmas decorations up on New Year's Day. This works well for me. By the time Christmas is over I am ready to get my house back in order after the holiday season. Taking down decorations, packing them away and having everything done by the beginning of the New Year feels good. It is a tradition that signifies the successful completion of the year, and a clearing and making ready for what is to come in the New Year.

Following you will find menus typical to what we serve for our traditional Christmas Day dinner and on New Year's Day.

Christmas or Hanukkah Menu

Roast Beef Prime Rib

With Roasted or Mashed Potatoes

Oven Roasted Brussel Sprouts

Horseradish-Cranberry Sauce

Roasted Beet & Goat Cheese Salad

New Year's Day Menu

Easy Slow Cooked Pork Roast with Sauerkraut

Mashed Potatoes

Pot of Greens

Black-eyed Peas

Corn Bread (Secret Recipe)

My Notes

My Notes:

Chapter 2

Appetizers & Snacks

While the family is gathering and waiting for the traditional holiday meal to be served, you'll have guests with a variety of appetites on different schedules. You will want to have some simple and healthy appetizers set out so they can help themselves while you are busy in the kitchen preparing the Traditional Holiday Menu items.

A big platter of crudities is wonderful for munching and can be prepared in advance. Add some cheeses, crackers, and dip to round things out. One of our family favorites is the Spicy Tomato Cheddar Spread which is delicious either on vegetables, with crackers, or made into mini-sandwiches on rye or pumpernickel bread. It can be made ahead and will last for several weeks when refrigerated. I usually make more than one batch because this Appetizer Recipe is so quick and easy and it makes an attractive hostess gift.

This variation of Traditional Chex Mix is a Family Favorite

Not just my own children but all of their friends ask for this each year. There are plenty of years that I make more than one of these large recipes.

HOLDAY PARTY MIX

MAKES 3 GALLONS

Ingredients

1 ½ Cups (3 Sticks) Butter
1 Tablespoon Garlic Powder
2 Teaspoons Onion Powder
2 Tablespoons Seasoned Salt
1 Cup Worcestershire Sauce
1 Box Wheat Chex Cereal
1 Box Rice Chex Cereal
1 Box Corn Chex Cereal
4 Cans Mixed Nuts (low salt)
1 Bag of Pretzels
1 Large Box Gold Fish Crackers
2 Bags of garlic-flavor bite-sized bagel chips, or regular size bagel chips broken onto 1 inch pieces.

Directions:

Preheat Oven to 250°

Melt butter in microwave; stir in seasonings. In a large bowl or bucket mix the remaining ingredients and pour the butter and seasoning mixture over top stirring gently until everything is evenly coated with the butter mixture. Pour the mixture into two large roasting pans. You will need to space the racks in your oven to accommodate both roasting pans—and I switch their position every time I stir the mixture. Bake one hour stirring every 15 minutes. Spread paper towels on your counter and pour the mixture on the paper towels to cool. Store in airtight containers, jars or gallon size zip lock freezer bags.

This dish is simple to make, delicious and makes and elegant presentation in its own bread bowl.

DILL CRAB DIP

MAKES 1 BREAD BOWL FULL OF DIP

Directions:

Preheat Oven to 375°

Cut 1 inch off the top of the bread and hollow out the loaf to make a bread bowl. Mix together the next six ingredients and put the mixture into the bread bowl.

Put the filled bread bowl on a cookie sheet and bake for approximately 10 minutes.

Serve warm with crackers or raw vegetables

Ingredients

1 loaf round bread from the deli
1-8 OZ package cream cheese
½ cup mayonnaise
1 Tablespoon prepared horse radish
1 Tablespoon Worcestershire sauce
2 Tablespoons chopped, fresh dill
6-8 ounces canned crab meat
Crackers or fresh raw vegetables

You can make this recipe in advance, and freeze the rolls wrapped in plastic wrap.

Take them out as needed, 1 day in advance to thaw. Slice & serve.

This is an excellent recipe to make in bulk and freeze to have on hand for unexpected guests, or to take as a dish to someone else's feast.

MEXICAN PINWHEELS

MAKES: 5 DOZEN

Ingredients

8 ounces shredded sharp cheddar cheese

½ cup, 0% fat, Greek yogurt

1 (4.5 ounce) can chopped green chilies, drained

1 (2 ¼ ounce) can sliced ripe olives, drained

2/3 cup chopped green onions

1/3 cup chopped fresh cilantro

1 clove garlic, crushed

¼ teaspoon seasoned salt

6 (9") whole wheat or sprouted grain tortillas

Directions:

Combine the first 9 ingredients. Spread about ½ cup of the mixture over each tortilla; roll up tortillas, jellyroll fashion. Wrap each roll separately in plastic wrap. Chill at least 3 hours.

Unwrap each roll and cut into ten slices. You may cut off and discard the ends if you choose.

This recipe is quick to make, portable, and can be made in advance.

It also makes a nice hostess gift. Package in an attractive jar and decorate the top with fabric and a ribbon.

SPICY TOMATO CHEDDAR SPREAD

MAKES 2.5 CUPS

Ingredients

16 oz sharp cheddar cheese, shredded

1 (4 oz) jar of chopped pimento, drained

1 (10-oz) can Rotel Original Diced Tomatoes & Green Chilies, drained

1 cup mayonnaise

1 teaspoon Worcestershire sauce

½ teaspoon salt

Directions:

Stir all the ingredients together in a bowl.

This recipe takes only 10 minutes to prepare.

It keeps quite well in the refrigerator and even gets better after a few days!

Great served on buttery round crackers and also makes a tasty variation of traditional Pimento Cheese on Rye sandwiches.

This is not only a great appetizer dish for the holiday, it is also a great dish for neighborhood gatherings and for your annual Superbowl Party!

HOT & SPICY CHICKEN DIP

FILLS A 9X13 INCH CASSAROLE DISH

Ingredients

3-4 boneless, skinless chicken breasts, baked & diced

1 bottle Texas Pete™ or Red Hot Wing Sauce

1 bottle (16 ounce) blue cheese salad dressing

1 (8-oz) block of cream cheese

1 (8-oz) block of cheddar cheese, shredded

Directions:

Preheat Oven to 350°

Spray a 9x13 inch casserole dish with cooking spray. Spread the diced chicken over the bottom of the casserole dish; pour the hot wing sauce over the chicken and stir.

Microwave the cream cheese until it is soft and mix it with the blue cheese dressing. Spread this mixture over the chicken mixture.

Bake for 20 minutes or until heated through.

Sprinkle shredded cheddar cheese over top and bake an additional 5 minutes.

Serve with tortilla chips.

CREAM CHEESE WITH SWEET PECAN TOPPING

MAKES 1 6-7 INCH SQUARE

Ingredients

2 (8-oz) packages cream cheese, softened

1.5 Tablespoons minced garlic

1.5 Tablespoons minced onion

¼ cup butter, melted

¼ cup brown sugar

1 cup finely chopped pecans

½ teaspoon prepared mustard

1 teaspoon Worcestershire sauce

Directions:

Combine the first three ingredients and shape into a one inch high square. Chill in the refrigerator for at least one hour.

Topping:

Mix the melted butter, brown sugar, pecans, prepared mustard and Worcestershire sauce together. Let cool for 5 minutes and then pour over the cream cheese square.

Cover and refrigerate.

Serve room temperature with crackers.

My Family Recipes—

My Family Recipes~

My Family Recipes~

My Family Recipes~

My Family Recipes~

Serves:

Ingredients:

Directions:

Chapter 3

Beverages

This recipe is so easy and it is a family favorite.

On Thanksgiving morning I put out a punch bowl full.

Adding a shot of spiced rum will also make it a delicious "adult beverage".

CITRUS PUNCH

MAKES 2 LITERS

Ingredients

1 (12 ounce can) frozen 5-Alive™ Concentrate

1 (2-liter) bottle of Ginger-ale

Optional: Slices of Orange, Lemon & Lime for Garnish

Directions:

Combine 5-Alive Concentrate & Ginger-Ale in a punch bowl and watch it disappear. It is recommended you have back up ingredients; you'll be refilling the punch bowl throughout the day.

Garnish with slices of orange, lemon and/or lime.

Optional: Prepare an ice ring ahead of time with cherries, lemons, limes & oranges.

Note: For an Adult Beverage, add a shot of spiced rum to your glass!

Such and elegant & delicious Adult Beverage!

Caution: They are also strong.

One Holiday Season I shared this recipe with several neighbors.

It was reported that a couple of them had guests that needed to spend the night with them after a few of these!

Chocolate Martinis

MAKES 1 ADULT BEVERAGE

Ingredients

1 ounce Vanilla Flavored Vodka

½ ounce Baily's Irish Crème

½ ounce Grand Marnier

½ ounce Godiva White Chocolate Liqueur

½ ounce Godiva Dark Chocolate Liqueur

Directions:

Fill a shaker glass with ice, pour all ingredients into the shaker over the ice. Shake vigorously.

Strain into a martini glass and serve.

Optional Garnishes:

Chill the martini glass and drizzle chocolate syrup, or chocolate topping that hardens into the glass.

Garnish with a peppermint stick.

This drink is also good served over ice.

This recipe came from my grandfather. We called it Shenandoah Road Eggnog because that was the name of the street he lived on. This eggnog recipe is strong enough that it may not need a glass. It is indeed a rich treat! You can tell this is an "old" recipe because there is no fear of the raw eggs! The alcohol does cook the eggs, however.

SHENANDOAH ROAD EGGNOG

MAKES 5 QUARTS

Ingredients

1 fifth of Whiskey (Bourbon or Rye)

1 pint light rum

1 pint whipping cream

2 quarts whole milk

10 eggs, separated

2 cups sugar

½ teaspoon salt

Fresh grated nutmeg

Directions:

Whip the whipping cream & once it is forming stiff peaks add 1 cup of sugar; set aside.

Beat egg whites until stiff; set aside.

Beat egg yolks; slowly add one cup of the whiskey, which cooks the eggs, while continuing to beat the mixture. Stir in one cup of sugar. Then, in order, add the whole milk, beaten egg whites, the remaining whiskey, rum, and whipped cream. If a power mixer is used, run on low speed. Add salt. Add nutmeg to taste &/or use as a garnish.

Note: If the eggnog is too strong it may be cut to the desired strength by adding more whole milk.

My Family Recipes~

Serves:

Ingredients:

Directions:

My Family Recipes~

Serves:

Ingredients:

Directions:

My Family Recipes~

Serves:

Ingredients:

Directions:

My Family Recipes~

Serves:

Ingredients:

Directions:

Chapter 4

Breads & Muffins

This recipe can be made in advance and frozen.

The smaller loaves make great gifts and they also travel well.

BANANA BREAD

MAKES 1 8"X4" LOAF or 2 4"x2" LOAVES

Ingredients

1 cup mashed ripe banana (about 2 bananas)

2/3 cup sugar

¼ cup vegetable oil

2 eggs

1 ¾ cups all-purpose flour

1 ¼ teaspoon cream of tartar

¾ teaspoon baking soda

½ teaspoon salt

Coconut Oil cooking spray

Directions:

Preheat Oven to 350°

Combine the first five ingredients in a large bowl and beat with a mixer at medium speed until smooth.

Combine flour, cream of tartar, baking soda and salt in a bowl, stirring with a fork. Add the flour mixture to the banana mixture, stirring just until moist. Spoon batter into an 8"x4" loaf pan coated with coconut oil cooking spray.

Bake at 350° for 40 minutes or until a wooden pick inserted in the center comes out clean. Cool 10 minutes in the pan on a wire rack; remove from pan. Cool completely on the rack.

Delicious & Nutritious

This is another recipe that can be made ahead of time & frozen.

Take out of the freezer the night before you want to serve them.

BREAKFAST MUFFINS

MAKES 12 MUFFINS

Ingredients

2/3 cup roasted sunflower seeds
½ cup whole wheat flour
½ cup all-purpose flour
1 teaspoon baking powder
½ teaspoon baking soda
½ teaspoon salt
1 teaspoon ground cinnamon
1 egg
2 Tablespoons vegetable oil
¾ cup grated carrot (about 2)
½ cup unsweetened applesauce
½ cup dark brown sugar
½ cup orange juice
1 teaspoon pure vanilla extract
½ cup raisins

Directions:

Preheat Oven to 375°

Line a muffin tin with paper liners or spray with cooking spray.

In a large bowl, mix together the sunflower seeds, whole wheat flour, all-purpose flour, baking powder, baking soda, salt & cinnamon. In a medium bowl, whisk the egg with the oil until smooth. Add the grated carrot, applesauce, brown sugar, orange juice, vanilla and stir until blended. Stir in the raisins. Add the flour mixture and mix just until combined, being careful not to over mix. Spoon into the 12 prepared muffin cups.

Bake 25 to 30 minutes. Muffins should be golden brown.

Refrigerate these muffins for up to one day or freeze for up to two weeks.

One of my Favorite Holiday Breakfast Breads!

Note: This recipe, as well as most of the loaf breads, can be made in advance and frozen.

CRANBERRY—ORANGE NUT BREAD

MAKES 1 8"X4" LOAF or 2 4"x2" LOAVES

Ingredients

- ¾ cup all-purpose flour
- ¾ cup whole wheat flour
- 1 teaspoon baking powder
- ¼ teaspoon salt
- ¼ cup unsalted butter, softened
- 2 large eggs
- ¼ cup orange juice
- 1 teaspoon grated orange peel
- ½ cup fresh or frozen cranberries, chopped & ½ cup walnuts, chopped

Directions:

Preheat Oven to 350°

Grease and flour loaf pan or pans.

In a small bowl combine the flours, baking powder and salt; set aside.

In a large bowl with an electric mixer at medium speed, beat butter and sugar until light and fluffy; continue beating as you add in the eggs, orange juice and orange peel. Mix thoroughly. Reduce the speed on the mixture to low and beat in the flour mixture just until blended. Fold in cranberries and walnuts.

Pour into loaf pan or pans. Bake 30 to 40 minutes or until a wooden pick inserted in the center comes out clean. Remove bread from pan to cool completely on a wire rack.

A Holiday Favorite.

They make wonderful gifts, wrapped & tied with a ribbon!

PUMPKIN BREAD

MAKES 2 8"X4" LOAF or 2 4"x2" LOAVES or 4 4"x2" LOAVES

Ingredients

½ cup 2% fat milk
2 1/3 Tablespoons vegetable oil
3 large eggs
2 cups fresh pumpkin puree OR 1 (15-ounce) can pumpkin
1 cup all-purpose flour
1 cup whole wheat flour
1 cup quick-cooking oats
1 cup sugar
2 teaspoons baking power
1/2 teaspoon baking soda
2 teaspoons ground cinnamon
½ teaspoon salt
1 cup raisins
¼ cup chopped pecans
Cooking spray

Directions:

Preheat Oven to 350°

Combine the milk, vegetable oil, eggs and pumpkin puree in a mixing bowl and stir well.

Combine flours and next six ingredients (flour—salt) in a large mixing bowl; add pumpkin mixture to flour mixture stirring just until moist. Fold in raisins and pecans.

Spoon batter into loaf pans coated with cooking spray. Bake at 350° for 50 minutes or until a wooden pick inserted in the center of the loaf comes out clean. Cool 10 minutes in the loaf pans on a wire rack; remove from the pans and cool completely.

Note: This recipe may be made ahead and frozen.

My Family Recipes ~

Serves:

Ingredients:

Directions:

My Family Recipes~

Serves:

Ingredients:

Directions:

My Family Recipes~

Serves:

Ingredients:

Directions:

My Family Recipes~

Serves:

Ingredients:

Directions:

My Family Recipes~

Serves:

Ingredients:

Directions:

Chapter 5

Breakfast Casseroles

This is one of my favorites.

I generally make it the morning after Thanksgiving.

The leftover Pudding makes delicious snacks!

APPLE CRANBERRY BREAKFAST PUDDING

MAKES 8—12 SERVINGS

Ingredients

4 cups skim milk

½ cup light brown sugar, firmly packed

½ teaspoon salt

6 ounces golden raisins

2 cups rolled oats

4-5 apples, cored, sliced thin, but not peeled

1 cup fresh cranberries, halved

1 cup chopped pecans, walnuts or almonds

¼ cup light brown sugar, firmly packed

0% fat Greek Yogurt

Cinnamon Sugar

Directions:

Preheat Oven to 350°

Combine milk, ½ cup brown sugar and salt in a large microwave-safe bowl. Heat in microwave until very hot but not boiling (about 6 to 8 minutes on high). To this mixture, add the raisins, oats, apples, cranberries coated with born sugar (to coat cranberries with brown sugar put both in a zip lock bag and shake), and nuts. Mix well. Place into a stoneware serving/cooking bowl and bake for 30 minutes.

Stir before serving.

Top each serving with a dollop of Greek Yogurt sweetened with cinnamon sugar.

Note: Use a crock pot with a removable stoneware insert for this dish. Then you can remove it from the oven and keep warm in the crockpot for late sleepers

Quick and easy way to have breakfast ready for a crowd.

This works especially well when not everyone wakes up at the same time.

BREAKFAST CASSEROLE

MAKES 6—8 SERVINGS

Ingredients

- **1 pound sausage**, browned and crumbled (or diced ham or cooked bacon, crumbled—or any combination of the three)
- **1 ½ cups (6 ounces) shredded longhorn cheese**
- **2 cups milk**, whole or 2%
- **6 slices of cubed whole wheat bread**
- **6 eggs, beaten**
- **1 teaspoon dry mustard**
- Optional: mushrooms, onions, green peppers

Directions:

Preheat Oven to 350° and spray the bottom of a 13"x9" casserole with cooking spray.

Mix all the ingredients together and pour into the Casserole dish. Bake uncovered for 45 minutes.

Note: *This dish may be mixed the night before and refrigerated overnight. This will help the flavors blend better, but it is not essential.*

Another great breakfast when you have a crowd.

Prepare and keep warm in a crock pot.

CHEESE GRITS CASSEROLE

MAKES 16 SERVINGS

Ingredients

8 cups water

2 teaspoons salt

2 cups uncooked quick-cooking grits

4 cups (16 ounces) sharp cheddar cheese

1 1/3 cups milk

2 teaspoons Worcestershire Sauce

8 large eggs, lightly beaten

2/3 cups butter

¼ teaspoon ground red pepper

¼ teaspoon paprika

Directions:

Preheat Oven to 350°

Bring water and salt to a boil in a large saucepan and stir in grits. Return to a boil, cover and reduce heat. Simmer 5 minutes stirring occasionally. Remove from heat and add cheese, milk, butter, Worcestershire sauce and ground red pepper, stirring until cheese and butter melt. Add eggs; stir well.

Spoon the mixture into a 4 quart casserole sprayed with cooking spray.

Sprinkle with paprika.

Bake uncovered at 350° for 1 hour or until thoroughly heated and lightly browned.

Let stand for 5 minutes before serving.

This is a family favorite with a special memory.

For years, until he passed away, Jay would make each family member a custom omelet on Thanksgiving morning. We'd have to get up early to put our name on his "omelet list", and he would cook in the order we signed up. This recipe reminds of us of Jay and his special contribution to our Holiday Festivities.

JAY'S OMELET CASSEROLE

MAKES 12 SERVINGS

Directions:

Preheat Oven to 325°

Cook the potatoes, ¾ cup green pepper, and onion in oil in a large skillet over medium—high heat, stirring constantly for about 8 minutes, until tender.

Combine the potato mixture, eggs, ham, 1 cup of tomato, salt and black pepper in a large bowl; stir well. Pour mixture into a 13x9 inch baking dish that has been coated with cooking spray.

Bake uncovered at 325° for 45 minutes or until center is solid and top is golden. Top with remaining green pepper, tomato & cheese and bake 5 more minutes or until the cheese melts.

Serve with Salsa on the side for garnish.

This filling casserole is all you need to serve at breakfast. Full of eggs, cheese, meat and vegetables, it's a meal in itself. Family Favorite thanks to many years of "Uncle Jay's Omelets."

Ingredients

3 cups frozen cubed hash brown potatoes
1 cup chopped green pepper, divided (reserve ¼ cup to sprinkle on top)
1/3 cup chopped onion
1 Tablespoon oil
18 large eggs, beaten
1 1/3 cups chopped tomato, divided (reserve ¼ cup to sprinkle on top)
2 1/3 cups chopped cooked honey baked ham
½ teaspoon salt
½ teaspoon black pepper
1 2/3 cups (6 ounces) shredded cheddar cheese
Salsa

I use this recipe when I need some additional variety!

It is one of the newer ones we've added to our collection.

EGGS BENEDICT CASSEROLE

MAKES 6—8 SERVINGS

Ingredients

12 eggs

2 cups half & half

1 Tablespoon chopped fresh parsley

1 teaspoon salt

1/ teaspoon garlic powder

½ teaspoon ground pepper

1 package English muffins, toasted and coarsely chopped

1 package of Canadian bacon, julienned

1 package hollandaise sauce mix
¼ cup melted butter
Zest of one lemon
1 Tablespoon lemon juice

Directions:

Preheat Oven to 350°

Spray a 13"x9" casserole dish with cooking spray.

Whisk together eggs, 1 cup of half & half, parsley, salt, pepper and garlic powder.

Combine muffins & bacon in the casserole dish and pour egg mixture over top.

Let the mixture set for 5 minutes.

Bake approximately 40 minutes until puffed and set.

Mix hollandaise sauce according to package directions using butter and remaining half and half. Stir in lemon juice and lemon zest.

Serve sauce with casserole.

My Family Recipes~

Serves:

Ingredients:

Directions:

My Family Recipes~

Serves:

Ingredients:

Directions:

My Family Recipes~

Serves:

Ingredients:

Directions:

My Family Recipes~

Serves:

Ingredients:

Directions:

Chapter 6

Cakes

Delicious and Easy to Make!

APPLE CAKE

MAKES ONE TUBE PAN

Ingredients

2 cups sugar

3 cups all-purpose flour

1 cup vegetable oil

3 eggs, well beaten

3 cups diced Granny Smith apples

1 teaspoon salt

1 teaspoon baking soda

2 teaspoons vanilla

1 cup chopped pecans

Frosting:

1 stick butter

1 ½ cups brown sugar

6 Tablespoons evaporated milk.

Directions:

Preheat Oven to 325°

Spray a tube pan with cooking spray.

Mix sugar, vanilla and oil together for several minutes; then add eggs and flour, reserving enough flour to coat nuts and apples. Coat the nuts and apples with the reserved flour; then add floured nuts and apples to the mixture. Beat well, and place in a greased tube pan and cook 1 ½ hours at 325°. Cool completely and frost with caramel frosting below:

Caramel Frosting:

Melt 1 cup butter; add 1 ½ cups brown sugar and let boil for 3 minutes. Add 6 Tablespoons of canned evaporated milk and cook 1 minute. Cool and spread on the cake.

Portable & Easy to Make

APPLE SHEET CAKE

MAKES 1 13"X9" SHEET CAKE

Directions:

Preheat Oven to 325°. **Coat a** 13x9 inch baking pan with cooking spray.

Combine flour, salt baking soda, cinnamon and nutmeg in a large bowl; stir with a fork. Add diced apple and chopped pecans; toss gently to combine. Make a well in the center of the mixture. Combine granulated sugar, applesauce, vanilla and eggs in a bowl and beat with a mixer at medium speed until well blended. Add to flour mixture and stir just until moist.

Spoon into the baking pan or casserole dish. Bake for 55 minutes or until a wooden pick inserted into the center comes out clean. Cool completely on a wire rack before frosting.

ICING: Beat butter and cream cheese with a mixer at medium speed until smooth. Add powdered sugar and teaspoon vanilla; beat just until blended. Spread icing over cooled cake.

Ingredients

3 cups all-purpose flour
1 teaspoon salt
1 teaspoon baking soda
1 teaspoon ground cinnamon
1 teaspoon ground nutmeg
2 cups diced Granny Smith apples
¼ cup chopped pecans
2 cups granulated sugar
1 cup unsweetened applesauce
1 teaspoon vanilla extract
3 large eggs
ICING:
½ cup butter, softened
1 8 ounce block cream cheese, softened
1 ½ cups powdered sugar
1 teaspoon vanilla extract

This recipe has been in my family for more than 4 generations; originating with my great-grandmother, Mary Eunice Lilly Davis. I can remember my grandmother always baked a cake using this recipe when we would come to visit. She would use either a chocolate frosting, or our favorite was Caramel Icing. You will find the recipe for Caramel Icing included in this section.

1-2-3-4 BASIC YELLOW CAKE

MAKES 3 8" LAYER CAKE ROUNDS

Ingredients

1 cup unsalted butter, softened

2 cups granulated sugar

3 cups all-purpose flour

4-6 eggs (I generally use six)

1 cup milk

2 teaspoons vanilla

3 teaspoons baking powder

¼ teaspoon salt

DIRECTIONS:

Preheat Oven to 350°. Grease and flour 3—8 inch cake pans and line the bottom of the pans with parchment paper.

Cream butter, sugar and vanilla together; add eggs one at a time beating together after each addition. Sift together flour, baking powder and salt. Add flour mixture alternately with milk.

Bake cake layers for approximately 30 minutes or until a wooden pick inserted in the center comes out clean.

Cool completely on a wire rack before frosting.

Note: For cupcakes, preheat the oven to 375° and cook cupcakes for 15 minutes.

This is a family favorite.

It can be made in a 12' round casserole dish, but we have always used a cast iron skillet.

PINEAPPLE UPSIDE DOWN CAKE

MAKES ONE 10" TO 12" ROUND CAKE

Directions:

Preheat Oven to 325°

Melt butter in a 12" cast iron skillet. Spread brown sugar over butter and arrange slices of pineapple, cherries and pecans over it.

Arrange one whole pineapple slice in the center, then arrange pineapple half slices around it with maraschino cherries in the center of each of the halves and in the center of the pineapple circle.

Pour the 1-2-3-4 Basic Yellow Cake batter over the pineapple slices in the skillet.

Bake for 40-45 minutes at 325° or until a wooden pick inserted into the center of the cake comes out clean.

When you remove the cake from the oven, turn it out upside down over a cake plate lined with parchment paper.

Ingredients

½ cup (1 stick) unsalted butter

1 cup brown sugar, firmly packed

1 can sliced pineapple, packed in its own juice

Maraschino cherries

Pecan halves

½ recipe of 1-2-3-4 Basic Yellow cake (on the previous page) substituting pineapple juice from the canned pineapple for milk

My grandmother, always did a lot of beating with a big cooking spoon after the butter melted. She said it helped to make it creamy. This frosting sets like chocolate fudge candy and the cooking time is tricky. If overcooked, the frosting will crack when you slice the cake. It tastes just as good though! My Grandmother used to use it on her 1-2-3-4 Basic Yellow cake; I like to frost the Tidewater Chocolate Pound Cake layers with this frosting.

CARAMEL ICING

MAKES FROSTING FOR A 2—LAYER CAKE

Ingredients

2 cups light brown sugar (one box)

¾ cup evaporated milk or cream*

¼ cup butter

1 teaspoon vanilla

Tiny pinch of salt

Directions:

Mix brown sugar and milk or cream. Allow to cook until it forms a soft ball in cold water. You can also use a candy thermometer to gauge the soft ball stage—240°. Remove from heat, add butter and beat vigorously. Add vanilla.

Spread on cake immediately.

This recipe is from my grandmother and the original recipe called for "top milk" which was the cream that would rise to the top of the bottle before milk was homogenized. I have always used evaporated milk for the recipe.

This is my favorite Chocolate Cake Recipe.

It is rich, delicious & versatile—Several Options are listed below.

My favorite is to make it a "Chocolate Praline Cake" by frosting it with Caramel Frosting.

TIDEWATER CHOCOLATE POUND CAKE

MAKES ONE TUBE PAN CAKE OR 2 8"or 9" ROUND LAYER CAKES

Directions:

Preheat Oven to 325°. Grease and flour 1 tube pan or 2 8" or 9" cake pans and line the bottom with parchment paper.

Cream butter, sugar and vanilla in a large mixing bowl for 5 minutes at medium speed. Add the eggs, one at a time, beating well after each addition. Dissolve the coffee granules in hot water; combine with buttermilk. Combine flour, cocoa, salt and baking powder. Add alternately with buttermilk mixture to creamed butter mixture, beating just until blended. Pour into greased and floured pan or pans.

Bake tube cake for 1 hour and 20 minutes; bake layer cakes for 45 minutes.

Options: *Sprinkle confectioner's sugar on top; Frost with Fluffy Cocoa Frosting (next page); Split the layers and put raspberry jam in—between; Frost with Caramel Icing (previous page)*

Ingredients

1 ½ cups butter, softened
3 cups sugar
2 teaspoons vanilla extract
5 eggs

2 teaspoons instant coffee granules
¼ cup hot water

1 cup buttermilk

2 cups un-sifted all-purpose flour
¾ cup cocoa powder

1 teaspoon salt
½ teaspoon baking powder

Use on 1-2-3-4 Basic Yellow Cake

Or

Tidewater Chocolate Pound Cake

FLUFFY COCOA FROSTING

MAKES ENOUGH TO FROST 1 CHOCOLTE POUND CAKE (SEE PREVIOUS PAGE)

Ingredients

¾ cup cocoa powder

4 cups (1 box) confectioners' sugar

½ cup unsalted butter

1 teaspoon vanilla extract

½ cup evaporated milk

DIRECTIONS:

Mix cocoa and sugar with butter. Blend in vanilla and milk. Add sugar a little at a time. Be careful not to over mix.

Frosts 1 two-layer cake or one tube cake.

Hostess Favorite!

Note: All layer cakes can be made ahead and frozen. If you frost them before freezing, let them freeze, then wrap with plastic wrap & foil until ready to serve. Unwrap them to allow them to thaw.

FAVORITE CARROT CAKE

MAKES 3 9—INCH LAYER CAKES

Ingredients

- 4 cups sifted cake flour
- 2 teaspoons baking powder
- 2 teaspoons ground cinnamon
- ½ teaspoon salt
- 3 cups granulated sugar
- 1 cup vegetable oil
- 5 eggs, lightly beaten
- 3 cups carrots, grated
- ½ cup golden raisins
- ½ cup dark raisins

DIRECTIONS:

Preheat Oven to 375°; butter and flour 3 9—inch round cake pans and line with parchment paper.

Sift together the cake flour, baking powder, baking soda, cinnamon and salt. Set aside.

In a large mixing bowl, beat the sugar, oil and eggs until light and fluffy. Stir in the grated carrots. Add the sifted dry ingredients and stir together by hand, folding in the raisins last.

Put the batter into the prepared pans and place in the oven. Reduce the temperature to 350°; bake for approximately 30 minutes or until a wooden pick inserted into the middle comes out clean. (The cakes should still be slightly moist in the center).

Cool the cake layers on a wire rack before removing from the pan.

Frost with Cream Cheese Icing (recipe on the following page).

Classic Frosting Recipe for Carrot Cake & Red Velvet Cake.

CREAM CHEESE FROSTING

MAKES ENOUGH TO FROST A 9" 3—LAYER CAKE

Ingredients

2 8—ounce packages cream cheese, softened

3 cups confectioners' sugar, sifted

12 Tablespoons (1 ½ sticks) unsalted butter

1 ½ cups solid vegetable shortening—white, not butter flavor

2 teaspoons vanilla

Directions:

Combine all ingredients in a large bowl and beat with an electric mixer at low speed for 3 minutes. Scrape the sides of the bowl and then beat on high for five minutes.

Spread the icing over a cooled cake.

Optional: Press one cup of finely chopped walnuts or pecans into the sides of the cake.

Family Favorite from Long Ago

This was my mother-in-law's recipe. I've never known anyone else who made Strawberry Shortcake this way. The cake is very dry, and the liquid from the strawberries and milk soften it up.

MIMA'S STRAWBERRY SHORTCAKE

MAKES 1—8" SQUARE SHORTCAKE

Directions:

Preheat Oven to 275°

Mix together Bisquick™, sugar, butter, milk and egg. Pour mixture into a greased 8—inch square pan.

Bake in a 275° oven for 30—35 minutes.

Cool.

To serve put a portion of cake in a bowl. Top with strawberries and milk.

Note: This cake is intentionally very dry—the topping will provide moisture.

Ingredients

1 ½ CUPS Bisquick™ baking mix

½ cup sugar

½ cup butter

½ cup milk

1 egg

TOPPING:

Strawberries, frozen OR Fresh Strawberries cut and sprinkled with sugar for syrup

Milk

This is a classic I discovered at "Harry's Farmer's Market" in Roswell, GA

Harry's became part of the Whole Foods Stores a couple of decades ago, and I am so glad I got the recipe before that happened!

SWEET POTATO, CHOCOLATE,

MAKES ONE 10 INCH TUBE CAKE

Ingredients

4—1 ounce squares semisweet chocolate

3 cups all-purpose flour

1½ cups granulated sugar

2 teaspoons baking powder

2 teaspoons baking soda

2 teaspoons ground cinnamon

1 teaspoon salt

¼ teaspoon freshly grated nutmeg

1 ½ cups vegetable oil

4 large eggs

1 cup pecans, coarsely chopped
1 teaspoon vanilla extract

Directions:

Preheat Oven to 350°; grease and flour a 10 inch tube pan.

Place chocolate in a small microwave bowl and cook on high 2 minutes until chocolate loses its shape when stirred; stir until smooth. Set aside.

In a medium size mixing bowl stir flour, sugar, baking powder, baking soda, cinnamon, salt and nutmeg to blend well; set aside.

In a large mixing bowl, with an electric mixer at medium speed, beat sweet potatoes and oil to blend well. Add eggs, one at a time; beat until thoroughly blended and smooth. Reduce speed to low; gradually beat in flour mixture to blend well. Stir in pecans.

Continued on next page ...

PECAN CAKE (continued)

Remove 1/3 of the batter to a medium size bowl; stir in melted chocolate and vanilla until smooth. Add batters by alternate spoonful's to the prepared tube pan; run a thin metal spatula or a knife at random through the batter to produce a marbled effect.

Bake 1 ¼ hours (75 minutes) or until a wooden pick inserted into the center comes out clean.

Let the cake cool in the pan on a wire rack for 10 minutes and then invert onto rack and remove from the pan. Cool cake completely.

If desired sprinkle cake with finely chopped pecans and confectioner's sugar to serve. *Note: To cook sweet potatoes, wash & scrub them with water and vegetable brush. Wrap the sweet potatoes individually in aluminum foil, pierce with a fork and bake at 450° for one hour. I generally start them cooking while I have something else cooking in the oven so I don't heat up the oven just for the potatoes. Let them cool, remove the skins d then mash.*

Ingredients

Continued from previous page ...

6 medium sweet potatoes, about 2 ½ pounds, cooked and mashed, OR two 17—ounce cans yams packed in syrup, drained and mashed, about 2 1/3 cups

1 ½ cups vegetable oil

4 large eggs

1 cup pecans, coarsely chopped

1 teaspoon vanilla extract

WHITE CHOCOLATE RASPBERRY CHEESECAKE

MAKES 1—9 INCH CHEESECAKE

Ingredients

Crust:
1 ½ cups Oreo Chocolate cookie crumbs
½ cup finely chopped pecans
1/3 cup melted butter

Filling:
4—8 ounce packages cream cheese, softened
8 ounces white chocolate
2 Tablespoons flour
½ teaspoon salt
1 ¼ cups sugar plus 2 Tablespoons extra
½ cup sour cream
1 Tablespoon vanilla
3 large eggs
1 package fresh raspberries (if using frozen, thaw & drain)

Directions:

Preheat Oven to 400°; Grease a 9 inch spring form pan with shortening.

Crust: Mix all crust ingredients and press the crust mixture into the bottom and sides of the pan. Bake about 10 minutes; remove from oven and reduce oven heath to 300°.

Filling: Melt white chocolate and set aside. Combine cream cheese, flour, salt and beat until very smooth and fluffy. Add 1 ¼ cups sugar, sour cream and vanilla—beat until well blended. Add eggs one at a time—beat until well blended.

Set 1/3 cup of the cream cheese mixture aside. Crush raspberries in a blender or food processor—add 2 Tablespoons of sugar. Add raspberries to small portion of cream cheese mixture.

Combine the melted white chocolate with the remaining cream cheese mixture—mix well. Pour in the cooled cookie crust. Drop large spoonful's of raspberry mixture randomly around in the pan; use a table knife to swirl. Bake 60 to 70 minutes at 300 degrees.

My Family Recipes~

Serves:

Ingredients:

Directions:

My Family Recipes~

Serves:

Ingredients:

Directions:

My Family Recipes~

Serves:

Ingredients:

Directions:

My Family Recipes~

Serves:

Ingredients:

Directions:

My Family Recipes~

Serves:

Ingredients:

Directions:

My Family Recipes~

Serves:

Ingredients:

Directions:

Chapter 7

Candies & Cookies

Family Favorite

This recipe was handed down from my mother and continues to be a favorite!

The secret ingredient is the peanut butter!

CHOCOLATE FUDGE CANDY

MAKES 1—8 INCH SQUARE PAN

Ingredients

3 Tablespoons butter

2 ounces bitter chocolate

2 cups granulated sugar

¾ cup cream or milk

2 teaspoons vanilla extract

2 Tablespoons smooth peanut butter

½ cup chopped pecans

Directions:

Butter an 8" square pan.

Melt butter and chocolate in a 2 quart saucepan on top of the stove. Add sugar and milk and mix. Boil, stirring occasionally, until mixture reaches the soft ball stage. Remove from heat, quickly add the vanilla, peanut butter and nuts—beat. Pour into an 8" square pan.

When thoroughly cooled or set, cut into one inch squares.

Use this version for your holiday baking.

It will give you enough for your Holiday Celebrations & some to give away as a gift.

It is recommended you use a candy thermometer with this size batch.

CHOCOLATE FUDGE CANDY LARGE BATCH

MAKES 2—13"X9" PANS FULL

Ingredients

¾ cup butter (1 ½ sticks)

8 ounces bitter chocolate

8 cups granulated sugar

3 cups cream or milk

2 Tablespoons plus 2 teaspoons vanilla extract

1/3 cup smooth peanut butter

2 cups chopped pecans

Directions:

Follow the instructions on the previous page, using a large stock pot to cook on the stove. With this amount of fudge it is much better to use a candy thermometer to determine when the candy has reached the sot ball stage (240°).

Premeasure and have ready in a bowl the peanut butter, vanilla and chopped nuts. Once this candy has reached the right temperature you will need to work quickly to add the remaining ingredients and pour in the pans to set.

Tip: I like to use portioned sized scoops for cookies.

This way all the cookies are the same size.

HOLIDAY COOKIES

MAKES 5 DOZEN 2 INCH COOKIES

Ingredients

2 cups all-purpose flour

¾ teaspoons baking soda

½ teaspoon salt

1 cup (8 ounces) softened butter flavored shortening

2/3 cup granulated sugar

½ cup firmly packed brown sugar

1 egg

1 teaspoon vanilla extract

12 ounce package (1¼ cups) M&M's Chocolate Candies in Red & Green Holiday Colors
¾ cup chopped nuts

Directions:

Preheat Oven to 375°

Combine flour, baking soda and salt; set aside.

Cream together shortening and sugars until light and fluffy; beat in egg and vanilla. Blend in flour mixture slowly. Stir in M&M's and pecans.

Drop by heaping teaspoonful's onto an ungreased cookie sheet.

Bake 8-11 minutes, until browned.

Cool 1 minute on cookie sheet; remove cookies from cookie sheet onto a wire rack to cool completely.

Delicious Chocolate Cookies with a spicy kick!

The secret ingredient in these little cookies is the cayenne pepper!

MEXICAN CHOCOLATE CHERRY ROUNDS

Directions:

Stir chocolate in top of double boiler over simmering water until smooth; cool.

Combine flour and next 5 ingredients in a medium bowl. Using an electric mixer, beat 1¾ cups sugar and butter in a large bowl until light and fluffy. Beat in eggs one at a time, then vanilla and chocolate. Gradually add dry ingredients, beating just until combined.

Cover and chill dough until firm, about 2 hours or overnight.

Preheat Oven to 350°.

Lightly butter a large cookie sheet. Form 1 inch round balls with the dough and roll in the powdered sugar and then press a cherry half into the top of each ball. Bake until cookies puff and crack but are still soft, about 10 minutes. Transfer to a wire rack to cool.; Store cookies at room temperature in an airtight container for up to one week or freeze up to one month.

Ingredients

6 ounces unsweetened chocolate, chopped

2 cups plus 2 Tablespoons all-purpose flour

1 Tablespoon ground cinnamon

2 teaspoons baking powder

1 teaspoon salt

¼ teaspoon cayenne pepper

¼ teaspoon cloves

1 ¾ cups sugar

¼ cup (1/2 stick) unsalted butter, softened

3 large eggs

1 teaspoon vanilla

2/3 cups confectioner's sugar

Dried cherry halves

I learned this recipe when I was a teenager.

It is a favorite and so easy to make!

NO BAKE COOKIES

MAKES 2 ½ DOZEN

Ingredients

½ cup (1 stick) butter

½ cup milk

2 cups granulated sugar

4 Tablespoons cocoa powder

3 cups quick cooking oats

1 teaspoon vanilla

½ cup smooth peanut butter

Directions:

Bring the butter, milk and sugar to a boil, then add remaining ingredients.

Drop by tablespoons onto parchment paper.

Cookies will harden as they cool, similar to fudge.

These Classic Cookies are a Desert Table Staple.

I've been baking them since I was a teenager.

PEANUT BUTTER COOKIES

MAKES 6 DOZEN

Ingredients

- 1 cup butter, softened
- 1 cup creamy peanut butter
- 1 cup granulated sugar
- 1 cup firmly packed brown sugar
- 1½ cups all-purpose flour
- 2 teaspoons baking soda
- ¼ teaspoon salt
- 1 teaspoon vanilla extract
- 2 Tablespoons extra sugar

Directions:

Preheat Oven to 375°

Beat butter and peanut butter at medium speed with an electric mixer until creamy; gradually add sugars, beating well. Add eggs and beat well. Combine flour, baking soda and salt in a medium bowl; add to butter mixture beating well. Stir in vanilla.

Cover and chill for three hours.

Shape into 1 ¼ inch balls; place 3 inches apart on an ungreased cookie sheet. Dip a fork in additional sugar; flatten cookies in a crisscross design.

Bake 7 to 8 minutes. Remove to a wire rack to cool.

I have to credit my English Girlfriend, Kay (who my children referred to as "the other Miss Kay") for this delicious recipe.

She brought over a plate one year and they were so delicious that we had to get the recipe. Teacakes were officially added to our collection.

TEACAKES

MAKES 2 ½ DOZEN COOKIES

Ingredients

1 cup butter, softened

½ cup confectioner's sugar, sifted

1 teaspoon vanilla

2 ¼ cups all-purpose flour, sifted

¼ teaspoon salt

¾ cup chopped nuts

Additional confectioner's sugar to roll cookies in after baking

Directions:

Preheat Oven to 400°

Cream butter, sugar and vanilla. Add flour and salt. Stir in nuts. Chill.

Roll into 1 inch balls and place on an ungreased cookie sheet. Bake at 400° for 10 to 12 minutes.

Remove from oven and roll in powdered sugar while warm; cool completely and roll in powdered sugar a second time.

Store in an air-tight container.

My Family Recipes~

Serves:

Ingredients:

Directions:

My Family Recipes–

Serves:

Ingredients:

Directions:

My Family Recipes~

Serves:

Ingredients:

Directions:

My Family Recipes~

Serves:

Ingredients:

Directions:

My Family Recipes~

Serves:

Ingredients:

Directions:

My Family Recipes ~

Serves:

Ingredients:

Directions:

Chapter 8
Pastries & Pies

Preparing Pie Crusts

Holiday pies are a family favorite! I recommend making homemade crusts using real, unsalted butter and whole wheat pastry flour. Pie crusts can be made ahead in bulk with an assembly line method, and it is so easy! This can be done with a food processor. Make several batches at a time to have all the crusts you need for the entire holiday season and you will only have to clean up once!

Use the pastry blade in the food processor. You will be making one 2-crust pie at a time. Put all the dry ingredients and the cold butter pieces into the food processor. Pulse for 8 to 10 seconds until the butter is cut in and the mixture looks like coarse meal. Then turn the processor on as you drizzle the cold water into the rest of the ingredients. As soon as the pastry forms a ball—this will take only a few seconds—the pastry is finished! Voila! It is that easy!

Now remove the pastry ball from the processor and cut in half. Make a ball out of each half and flatten. You can wrap the pastry balls individually in plastic wrap and freeze them. Repeat for as many pie crusts as you anticipate you may need for the holiday season.

 Another method that I like even better if you have the storage space in your freezer is to go ahead and roll out the pastry for the pie pan. If you roll the pastry out, cover with parchment paper and layer the pastries in a clean pizza box. Go to your local pizza place and ask them for a box. I've always been able to get a free box just for the asking. The size for a 12" pizza is perfect!

When you are ready to bake your pies, take out as many crusts as you need to thaw while you are preparing the filling.

Don't forget to make a few extra crusts for decorations. I like to use small cookie cutters in the shape of leaves, pumpkins or whatever is appropriate for the season, and use them to decorate the crust. This is sure to make your pie look special!

All-purpose flour can be substituted.

If you don't want to make your own crust then buy prepared crusts in the refrigerator section of your grocery store.

WHOLE WHEAT PIE CRUST

MAKES 1—9" DOUBLE CRUST PIE PASTRY

Directions:

Food Processor Method:

Combine flour, salt and sugar in a food processor and process for a few seconds to mix. Add butter; process until mixture resembles coarse meal, about 8 to 10 seconds.

Add ice water in a slow steady stream through the feed tube of the food processor, with machine running, until dough holds together for no longer than 30 seconds.

For Hand Method:

For hand method, place dry ingredients in a large bowl. Add butter; blend with a pastry cutter until mixture resembles coarse meal.

Mix dough with a wooden spoon, adding water until dough just holds together.

Turn dough out onto a piece of plastic wrap. Divide in half and press each piece into a flat circle. Wrap in plastic wrap. Refrigerate for at least 1 hour before rolling out into a pie crust.

Ingredients

2 ½ cups organic whole wheat pastry flour

1 teaspoon salt

1 teaspoon granulated sugar

1 cup (2 sticks) cold unsalted butter, cut into small pieces

¼ - ½ cup water

Classic Recipe

Optional: Additional 2 teaspoons sugar and ½ teaspoon cinnamon

APPLE PIE

MAKES 1—9 INCH PIE

Ingredients

Pastry for 2 crust pie

6 cups (1 ½ pounds) peeled, sliced cooking apples

1 Tablespoon lemon juice

½ cup granulated sugar

½ cup firmly packed brown sugar

2 Tablespoons all-purpose flour

½ teaspoon cinnamon

¼ teaspoon nutmeg

2 Tablespoons unsalted butter

1 egg yolk

Directions:

Preheat Oven to 450°

Roll half of pastry to 1/8—inch thickness on a lightly floured surface. Place in a 9-inch pie plate; set aside.

Combine apple and lemon juice in a 2 quart saucepan. Combine ½ cup sugar and next 5 ingredients, mixing well. .Spoon over apple mixture, tossing gently. Cook over medium heat until apples become soft. Spoon filling evenly into pastry shell.

Roll remaining pastry to 1/8-inch thickness; transfer to top of pie. Trim off excess pastry along edges. Fold edges under and crimp.Cut slits in top crust for steam to escape. Brush pastry lightly with beaten egg yolk. If desired, combine 2 teaspoons sugar and 1/8-teaspoon cinnamon to sprinkle on pie. Cover the edges of pastry with aluminum foil to prevent excessive browning. Bake at 450 degrees for 15 minutes; reduce heat to 350 degrees and bake 50 more minutes. Remove to wire rack to cool.

Classic Recipe with a Holiday Twist!

CRAN-APPLE PIE

MAKES 1—9 INCH PIE

Ingredients

Pastry for 1 crust pie

4 cups peeled, sliced cooking apples, or about 4 large apples
2 cups fresh cranberries
¾ cups sugar
¼ cup all-purpose flour
¼ cup firmly packed brown sugar
½ teaspoon ground cinnamon
¼ teaspoon ground nutmeg

TOPPING:

½ cup all-purpose flour
1/3 cup firmly packed brown sugar
¼ teaspoon ground cinnamon
Dash of freshly ground nutmeg
¼ cup unsalted butter

Directions:

Preheat Oven to 375°

Roll half of pastry to 1/8—inch thickness on a lightly floured surface. Place in a 9-inch pie plate; set aside.

Filling:

Combine apple & cranberries in a large bowl. Combine ¾ cup sugar and next r ingredients; add to apple mixture, tossing gently. Spoon into pastry shell.

Topping:

Combine ½ cup flour and next 3 ingredients; stir mixture well. Cut in butter with a pastry blender until mixture is crumbly. Stir in pecans. Sprinkle crumb mixture over apple mixture.

Bake at 375° for 45 minutes.

Serve warm or at room temperature.

Family Favorite.

Freeze fresh blackberries in the summer for this or use frozen berries.

This is also an excellent summer pie recipe & blueberries can be substituted for blackberries.

BLACKBERRY PIE

MAKES 1—9 INCH PIE

Ingredients

Pastry for 2 crust pie

1 cup sugar

1½ Tablespoons flour

1 Tablespoon lemon juice

4 cups blackberries, fresh or frozen

¼ teaspoon almond extract

2 2/3 Tablespoons quick cooking tapioca

Directions:

Preheat Oven to 450°

Line a 9-inch ceramic pie pan with ½ pastry crust. Keep pastries refrigerated while making filling. Preheat oven to 450 degrees.

Filling:

Combine blackberries, sugar, lemon juice, almond extract and tapioca. Pour into pie crust and dot with butter. Top with remaining pastry crust.

Bake in a 450° oven for 10 minutes. Reduce heat to 350° and continue cooking 40 minutes.

Remove pie to a wire rack to cool.

This recipe was found on the bottom of a ceramic pie plate.

I adjusted it to our taste; our Family Favorite blackberry pie is a version of this recipe.

CHERRY PIE

MAKES 1—9 INCH PIE

Ingredients

Pastry for 2 crust pie

1 ½ cups granulated sugar

1 2/3 Tablespoons unsalted butter

1 Tablespoon fresh lemon juice

4 cups tart cherries, fresh or frozen, pitted

¼ teaspoon almond extract

2 2/3 cup quick cooking tapioca

Directions:

Line a 9-inch pie plate with ½ pastry crust. Keep pastries refrigerated while making filling.

Preheat oven to 450°.

Filling:

Combine cherries, sugar, lemon juice, almond extract and tapioca. Pour into pie crust and dot with butter. Top with remaining pastry crust.

Bake in a 450° oven for 10 minutes. Reduce heat to 350° and continue cooking 40 minutes.

Remove the pie to a wire rack for cooling.

Old Family Favorite.

When I was a teenager my dad used to ask me to make this pie for him.

CHOCOLATE MINT PIE

MAKES 1—8 TO 9 INCH PIE

Ingredients

CRUST:

30 vanilla wafers

2/3 cup unsalted butter

FILLING:

½ cup unsalted butter, softened

1 cup confectioner's sugar

2 squares unsweetened chocolate, melted

2 eggs

1/8 teaspoon peppermint extract

1 teaspoon vanilla extract

TOPPING:

½ pint heavy cream

¼ cup sugar

Directions:

Crust:

Finely crush the vanilla wafers. Melt 2/3 cup butter and combine with crumbs. Line buttered pie pan with mixture and chill at least one hour.

Filling:

Cream ½ cup butter. Add sugar and continue creaming. Gradually add chocolate, which has been melted and cooled. Add eggs, stirring well after each addition. Stir in peppermint and vanilla extracts. Place the filling in the shell, and chill for several hours.

Topping:

Whip heavy cream until it becomes stiff. Add sugar and 1 teaspoon of vanilla extract.

When serving, top with whipped cream topping.

Optional: Crush peppermint sticks and sprinkle on top of whipped topping for decoration.

Five Star Family Favorite.

Confession: I often catch family members eating a slice of this pie at breakfast.

CUSTARD PIE

MAKES 1—9 INCH PIE

Ingredients

1—9" pastry shell

4 eggs, slightly beaten

½ cup sugar

½ teaspoon vanilla extract

¼ teaspoon salt

2 ½ cups milk

Freshly grated nutmeg

Directions:

Pre-bake pastry shell for 5 minutes in a 350° oven.

Mix together eggs, sugar, vanilla, salt and milk and pour into pre-baked pie crust. Sprinkle generously with nutmeg.

Bake in a 350° oven for 60-65 minutes.

Pecan Pie is so rich an entire slice is generally too much.

I like making these squares as an alternative because they are more portion friendly.

PECAN PIE SQUARES

MAKES 2 ½ DOZEN

Ingredients

CRUST:

1 ¾ cups all-purpose flour

1/3 cup firmly packed light brown sugar

¾ cup butter

FILLING:

1 cup brown sugar

4 large eggs

1 cup dark corn syrup

¼ cup butter, melted

1 teaspoon vanilla extract

1/8 teaspoon salt

1 ¼ cups chopped pecans

Directions:

Crust:

Combine flour and brown sugar; cut in butter with a pastry blender until crumbly. Press mixture evenly into a greased 13x9-inch pan. Bake at 350 degrees for 15-17 minutes.

Filling:

Combine 1 cup brown sugar and next 5 ingredients, stirring well. Stir in pecans. Pour filling over prepared crust. Bake at 350 degrees for 35 minutes or until set. Cool in pan on wire rack. Cut into bars or squares.

Note: The advantage of making pecan pie this way is that you can have a small portion and enjoy!

Holiday Memories: One year two of our nephews had a pumpkin pie eating contest. The first one to eat ½ of the pie and whistle won. The younger brother won with a time of 3 minutes and 38 seconds.

CLASSIC PUMPKIN PIE

MAKES 1—8 TO 9 INCH PIE

Directions:

Preheat the oven to 450°. Put unbaked pie shell into pie pan and refrigerate while you are making the filling.

Mix all the remaining ingredients together and pour into the unbaked pie shell. Generously top with nutmeg. Bake at 450 degrees for 10 minutes, then reduce the oven temperature to 325 degrees and bake an additional 40-45 minutes. When filling is done it will not adhere to a knife when inserted in the center of the pie.

Cool and refrigerate. Serve topped with whipped cream.

Ingredients

1—9" unbaked pie shell

1 ½ cups pumpkin puree or canned pumpkin

¾ cups sugar

½ teaspoon salt

1 teaspoon cinnamon

½ teaspoon nutmeg

3 eggs

1 Tablespoon flour

1 teaspoon vanilla extract

2 cups half-and-half

Variation on a theme.

Funny how some folks who don't like sweet potatoes or sweet potato casserole still love this pie!

ORANGE SWEET POTATO PIE

MAKES 1—9 INCH PIE

Ingredients

Orange crust (see the following page for recipe)

3 large eggs, beaten

1 cup granulated sugar

2 cups cooked, sweet potatoes put through a ricer and mash (2-3 large sweet potatoes)

1/3 cup milk
1/3 cup half-and-half

¼ cup butter, melted

1 Tablespoon orange juice

1 teaspoon vanilla extract
1/8 teaspoon lemon extract

Generous pinch ground nutmeg

Directions:

Preheat oven to 350°.

In a medium bowl combine eggs, sugar and sweet potatoes; beat well. Mix in milk and half-and-half. Blend in butter, orange juice, vanilla and lemon extracts, and nutmeg. Pour into chilled orange crust (recipe for orange crust can be found on the following page).

Bake 40-45 minutes or until knife inserted in center of the filling comes out clean.

Note: Serve with a dollop of whipped cream and a cup of rich coffee on the side.

Crust for Sweet Potato Pie

ORANGE CRUST

MAKES 2—9 INCH CRUSTS

Directions:

Sift flour and salt into a large bowl. Cut in butter, shortening and orange rind until mixture is the texture of coarse meal.

In a small bowl, combine 5 Tablespoons of Orange Juice, sugar and nutmeg. Using a fork, work orange juice mixture into flour until ingredients hold together. Gradually add additional orange juice, if necessary.

Form into a ball, cover with plastic wrap and let rest 10 minutes.

Divide dough in half. On floured surface roll out half of dough into a circle. Place in a 9" pie plate and gently flute the edges.

Repeat with the remaining dough, freeze 20 minutes, wrap well and freeze for future use.

Ingredients

2 2/3 cups all-purpose flour

½ teaspoon salt

1 stick (4 ounces) unsalted butter cut into small pieces

½ cup chilled shortening, cut into small pieces

1 teaspoon grated orange rind

5—7 Tablespoons chilled orange juice

2 teaspoons granulated sugar

1/8 teaspoon ground nutmeg

My Family Recipes~

Serves:

Ingredients:

Directions:

My Family Recipes~

Serves:

Ingredients:

Directions:

My Family Recipes~

Serves:

Ingredients:

Directions:

My Family Recipes~

Serves:

Ingredients:

Directions:

My Family Recipes~

Serves:

Ingredients:

Directions:

Chapter 9

Holiday Entrees

Turkey & Trappings

Prime Rib

Slow Cooker Pork

PREPARING A TURKEY

Thanksgiving just wouldn't be the same without the Turkey and there are many ways to prepare & cook a Turkey. I've experimented with roasting the turkey with many recipes including brining and basting with various mixes. Our family has also fried our turkey. Each method can produce a delightful bird with moist and flavorful meat. Choosing the best option for preparing your Turkey will depend on how many people you are cooking for, how much oven space you have, and whether you would like to have leftovers to use in other recipes after the traditional dinner. You DO want leftovers! There are some delicious recipes in this book for using the leftover turkey. You will find my favorite recipes and tips for both roasting and frying your turkey on the following pages.

ROASTING YOUR TURKEY

Roasting a turkey in the oven is the most traditional way to prepare the turkey. You will find a recipe for roasting the turkey with specific instructions on storing your turkey, preparing the turkey for roasting, and how to ensure a moist golden roasted bird. Cooking your turkey with stuffing inside is not recommended due to safety concerns. Instead, try stuffing your bird with fresh root vegetables to ensure it stays moist and cooks evenly. Use vegetables such as onions, potatoes, turnips, carrots and parsnips. It is recommended you baste the turkey in a mixture of dry white wine and butter.

If you do not have a meat thermometer then go buy one. It is a good investment. Be certain you roast your turkey until the temperature on the thermometer reaches at least 180 degrees when placed into the thigh. If you would like extra white meat you can roast an additional breast in the oven with your whole turkey.

FRYING YOUR TURKEY

Frying a turkey is another excellent method of preparing your holiday bird. We began frying the turkey when our family gatherings got so big that it was virtually impossible to supply our feast using just one bird. Frying a turkey is much faster than roasting it in the oven, which helps free up the oven for other holiday items to be cooking, and it always produces a delicious and moist bird. Just like grilling, it ends up being a fun event for those who are preparing and cooking the bird, or birds, for the feast. We've included a recipe which explains just how to prepare your turkey for frying. The directions will explain the type of oil you need, the right temperature and everything you need to know if you are frying a turkey for the first time. Safety is important, so follow all of the rules. So long as you follow the rules you should have fun with frying your turkey and everyone will be raving about the result!

TRAPPINGS FOR THE TURKEY

Along with the Traditional Turkey Recipes, there are side dishes which are essential to a traditional Holiday Turkey Feast. I like to make my turkey gravy ahead of time with homemade chicken broth, a few turkey legs or wings and roasted vegetables. This way all I need to do is thaw and heat on the day of the Feast. I generally keep the gravy warm in a 2 Quart Crock Pot. You will find a recipe for "Make Ahead Turkey Gravy" in this chapter. Homemade cranberry sauce can be made in advance as well. Dressing for the turkey is a must, whether you like the traditional bread dressing or the more southern version using cornbread in the recipe. Be sure you dry your own bread cubes for this recipe. The dressing will taste so much better and your kitchen will smell yummy during the drying process!

Whether you choose to roast or fry your bird you will find a delicious recipe in *Your Holiday Feast* cookbook, along with instructions on how to handle, prepare, cook and carve your bird.

Let's talk some more turkey …

TURKEY FAQ'S

What size Turkey should you buy?

Allow about 1 pound per person. If you want to allow enough to have some leftovers, and who doesn't—we have some delicious recipes for using leftover turkey in *Your Holiday Feast*—you will want to allow for even more—our favorites are Hot Brown Sandwiches and Turkey Alfredo. When our family got large enough that just ONE turkey wouldn't feed us all we started frying our turkeys—this method cooks a turkey weighing up to about 14 pounds very quickly so we could do more than one. It also keeps the oven free for other things that need cooking.

Our family is partial to White Meat. Which turkey will give the most breast meat?

As a rule, the larger the turkey, the larger proportionally the breast. Surprisingly, this means that toms (16 pounds or over) average more breast for their size than hens. You can also roast an additional whole or half turkey breast in to oven alongside the whole turkey to add to amount of white meat.

For dark meat lovers, "Can I roast extras with the turkey?"

Sure you can! Just follow the cooking guide on the package for timing, arranging extra drumsticks and thighs around the turkey in the roasting pan.

When should I purchase a fresh Thanksgiving turkey & how long can I store it?

Home refrigerators are designed for family use. Since it is opened and closed often it is impossible to keep the turkey uniformly cold. This is why you should purchase a fresh turkey only 1-2 days before cooking it unless you have a refrigerator that is designated for extra storage and isn't opened frequently. Alternately, if you must bring a fresh turkey home earlier than that, you can keep it colder without freezing it by moving it back and forth at 12-hour intervals from freezer to refrigerator. When storing your turkey in the refrigerator, it should be kept in the coldest part of the refrigerator, on a low shelf toward the back.

What does the sell-by date mean on a fresh turkey?

The sell-by date is the last day on which the turkey can be sold as a fresh product. It also means you can safely purchase it on that date and either prepare or freeze it. If you purchase the turkey before the sell-by date, follow the recommendations above for storing it.

Is it still considered safe to stuff a turkey?

I recommend preparing your dressing separately in a casserole dish. I stuff the cavity of the bird with large vegetables for moisture and flavor and to help the turkey cook evenly. When doing this, used onion quarters, carrots, celery and parsnips—most any root vegetables will do.

How long should I allow for roasting a turkey?

Ovens vary, but as a general rule you can figure about 15-20 minutes per pound for a bird under 16 pounds and 12 to 15 minutes for birds 16 pounds and over. The guide below estimates cooking times; please use a cooking thermometer along with the guidelines below to test for doneness.

POUNDS	APPROXIMATE COOKING TIME
8—12	2 ¾ to 3 hours
12—16	3 to 3 ¾ hours
16—20	3 ¾ to 4 ¼ hours
20—24	4 ½ to 5 hours

How do I know when the turkey is done?

Overcooking causes dryness—so you do not want to over-cook your turkey but you must be certain it is cooked completely for safety. Here are some checks for doneness—the most reliable method to check for doneness is to use a meat thermometer.

- The thermometer in the bird pops up. Many birds come with a thermometer inserted and when it pops up this means the bird is done.

- The juices from the bird run clear.

- The joints, such as the drumstick, move easily

- A meat thermometer inserted into the thickest part of the breast registers 170 degrees or if you insert it into the thickest part of the thigh it will register 180 degrees.

How can I make sure the turkey stays moist?

Brush the skin with butter & baste every 30 minutes during cooking. You can also put a cup of water in the roasting pan when you start cooking the turkey. Since the breast cooks faster than the rest of the turkey you can cover it with foil or cheese cloth (soaked in butter and wine) until the last hour.

How do I carve a turkey?

After roasting the turkey allow it to stand at room temperature at least 20 minutes to allow the juices to be drawn back into the meat and make carving easier. Use a sharp carving knife and fork.

Remove the drumsticks and thighs on both sides by pulling the leg away from the body and cutting through the skin to reach the meat and expose the joint. Sever the thigh at the hip joint where it meets the body. Separate the drumsticks from the thighs at the connecting joint.

Hold the drumstick at the knobby end and cut downward around the bone to slice the meat. Hold the thigh with a long carving fork and carve away the meat parallel to the bone.

Cut off the wings at the shoulder joints.

Hold the breast firmly with the carving fork. One side at a time, make a horizontal base cut parallel to the table down near the wing; then cut down along the breast to carve it into thin slices. Every slice will stop at the parallel base cut.

Chicken Broth can be made weeks in advance and frozen in airtight containers. Use part of the broth for "Make Ahead Turkey Gravy" and freeze the rest to use in the dressing for Thanksgiving dinner. Sometimes it is just as easy to make a double batch and have broth for the entire winter season. Freeze it in 4 cup containers and thaw and use as needed. I use the cooked meat to make Chicken Enchilada Casserole.

CHICKEN BROTH

MAKES 16 CUPS

Ingredients

1 whole chicken, cleaned and cut up into pieces
12 cups water; add more later as needed
½ bunch celery, washed and stalks cut into 2"-3" pieces
4 onions, peeled and cut into fourths
4 carrots, peeled and cut lengthwise and then cut into 2" to 3" pieces
1 bunch parsley, curly or Italian
2-3 cloves garlic, minced
Fresh thyme and rosemary, if available
1 teaspoon salt
½ teaspoon whole peppercorns OR ½ teaspoon freshly ground pepper
2 bay leaves
A few dashes of poultry seasoning &/or ground thyme

Directions:

Combine all ingredients in a large stock pot and bring to a boil. Reduce to simmering and let simmer for about 4 hours.

Chicken pieces can be removed after the first 45 minutes, cooled and meat removed from the bones for use in other recipes. (Check out our recipe for Chicken Enchiladas)

When cooking is complete, remove vegetables and strain. If refrigerator space allows, chill overnight & remove fat.

Thaw gravy the day before your Holiday Dinner. Keep it warm in a crock pot. On the day of your holiday dinner, after the turkey is cooked and removed from the roasting pan, you can add the pan drippings to the heated gravy for additional flavor.

MAKE-AHEAD TURKEY GRAVY

MAKES 8 CUPS

Directions:

Preheat oven to 400°. Arrange wings in a single layer in a large roasting pan; scatter onions and carrots over top. Roast 1 ¼ hours or until wings are browned.

Put wings, onions and carrots into a large pot. Add water to roasting pan and stir to scrape up any brown bits on the bottom and add to the pot. Add 6 cups broth and the thyme. Bring to a boil, reduce heat and simmer uncovered for 1 ½ hours.

Remove the wings to a cutting board. When cool, pull off the skin and the meat. Discard skin and save the meat for another use. Use a strainer & strain the broth into a 3 quart saucepan, pressing the vegetables to extract as much liquid as possible. Discard vegetable. Skim fat off broth. Whisk flour into the remaining 2 cups broth until smooth.

Bring the broth in the saucepan to a gentle boil. Whisk in flour mixture and boil 3-4 minutes to thicken and remove floury taste. Stir in butter and pepper. Serve or pour into containers and refrigerate up to one week or freeze in airtight containers for up to 3 months.

Ingredients

4 turkey wings (approximately 3 pounds)

2 medium onions, peeled and quartered

1 cup water

8 cups chicken broth

2-3 carrots, sliced horizontally and cut into 2-3 inch pieces

½ teaspoon dried thyme

¾ cup all-purpose flour

2 Tablespoons butter

½ teaspoon freshly ground pepper

Cranberry sauce can be made several days in advance – it keeps as well as any jelly or preserve. You can make one batch and it will keep throughout the holiday season. It also makes a good hostess gift!

I also serve this with along with Horseradish Sauce with a Standing Prime-Rib Roast for our Christmas Holiday Feast.

CRANBERRY SAUCE

MAKES 2 ½ CUPS

Ingredients

2 Oranges

1 cup sugar

¾ cups water

½ teaspoon freshly grated nutmeg

1 teaspoon vanilla

12 ounces of whole fresh cranberries

Directions:

Zest the two oranges and juice them. Combine the orange zest, orange juice, sugar, water, nutmeg and vanilla in a saucepan and heat until boiling. This will make syrup. Add the fresh cranberries and simmer for approximately 12 minutes. Remove from heat, place in an attractive jar, cool and refrigerate.

Family Favorite

Classic Family Recipe

ESSENTIAL BREAD DRESSING

MAKES 8—10 SERVINGS

Ingredients

1 loaf white bread

1 loaf soft whole wheat bread

2-3 celery stalks, diced

1 large onion, diced

½ cup (1 stick) unsalted butter

2 eggs, beaten

2 - 4 cups of chicken broth

Salt, pepper, poultry seasoning to taste

Directions:

1 to 2 weeks prior to "the big dinner"

Break or cut bread into cubes. Put in a large uncovered container or into two or more bowls for drying. Stir cubes every day so they dry out thoroughly.

The day of the meal:

Sauté celery and onion in melted butter for a few minutes. In a large mixing container sprinkle dried bread cubes with seasonings and toss. Add butter-onion-celery mixture and mix. Add eggs and mix. Add chicken broth a little at a time and mix until it is a soft, sticky (but not gummy) consistency. Taste to check for correct seasoning amounts; add more spices if needed. Place in a large baking dish which has been sprayed with vegetable cooking spray. Cover with aluminum foil and bake at 325 degrees for one hour. Remove cover and bake for an additional 15 minutes or more, or until it looks good enough to eat!

Best eaten with turkey and gravy!

ROASTED TURKEY

MAKES 14—16 SERVINGS

Ingredients

1 20 to 21 pound fresh whole turkey, giblets (the heart, gizzard and liver) and neck removed from the cavity, turkey rinsed with cool water, and dried with a paper towel.

1 ½ cups (3 sticks) melted unsalted butter plus

4 Tablespoons unsalted butter at room temperature

1 bottle dry white Madeira wine

2 teaspoons coarse salt – sea salt or kosher salt

2 teaspoons freshly ground pepper

Directions:

Let the turkey stand at room temperature for 1-2 hours

Place the rack on the lowest level in your oven. Preheat oven to 450 degrees. In a medium bowl combine melted butter and white wine fold a large piece of cheesecloth into quarters. Make a 17" square of several layers – immerse the cheesecloth in the butter & wine mixture to soak.

Working on a large piece of parchment paper, fold the wing tips under the turkey. Sprinkle salt and pepper inside the turkey. Fill large cavity and neck cavity loosely with the chopped vegetables and ½ of the herbs – do not pack tightly. Tie the legs together loosely with kitchen string. A bow is easy to undo later and it is not necessary to make a tight knot). Fold the neck flap under and secure with toothpicks. Rub the turkey all over with the softened butter.

Use a heavy metal roasting pan with sides 2-3 inches high. Place remaining vegetables in the bottom of the pan. Place the roasting rack on top of the vegetables, then place the turkey, breast side up, on the roasting rack. Sprinkle the turkey with the remaining salt and pepper.

ROASTED TURKEY, continued

Lift the cheesecloth out of the liquid and gently squeeze it, leaving it very damp. Spread the folded cheesecloth evenly over the breast and down the sides of the turkey, covering some of the leg area. If you have a large oven place the turkey, legs first into the oven. If your roasting pan will only fit sideways in your oven, turn the pan every hour so the turkey cooks evenly. Cook for 30 minutes, then using a pastry brush baste the cheesecloth and all exposed parts of the turkey with the butter & wine mixture. Reduce the temperature to 350 degrees & cook 2 ½ more hours, basting with a pastry brush every 30 minutes. Watch the pan juices – if the pan gets too full, spoon out some of the juices so the level remains below the rack.

After the third hour of cooking, remove and discard the cheesecloth. Turn roasting pan so the breast faces the back of the oven. Baste your turkey with the juices that have accumulated in the bottom of the pan. If there are not enough juices, continue to use the butter and wine mixture. The skin gets fragile as it browns, so baste carefully, particularly over the breast area. Cook 1 more hour.

Continued on next page…

Ingredients

Continued...

Vegetables to fill the cavity – choose from:

onion, celery, parsnip, turnip, carrot

Fresh poultry herbs – rosemary, thyme and sage

1 package unbleached cheesecloth

Use paper towels when preparing the turkey. Any dishcloth or towels you might touch while preparing the raw turkey should go straight into the laundry.

ROASTED TURKEY, continued …

An instant-read thermometer is a good investment if you do not have one. When feeding a large part you do not want to be guessing if your turkey is done or not.

After the fourth hour of cooking, insert an instant-read thermometer into the thickest part of the thigh. Do not poke the thermometer into a bone. The thermometer should reach at least 180 degrees and the turkey should be golden brown. The breast does not need to be checked for temperature. If the turkey is not golden brown or does not register 180 degrees, baste the turkey and return it to the oven and cook for another 20 to 30 minutes or until the instant read thermometer reaches 180 degrees.

When the turkey is fully cooked, transfer it to a platter and let it rest 20-30 minutes before carving.

Note:

If you need the oven for other items after the turkey is cooked and you need it to rest for longer than 30 minutes you can cover it with foil and place a large bath towel over top to hold the heat in until it is time to carve it.

When our family got large enough that we needed more than one bird for our holiday dinner we began frying them because of the faster cooking time.\

This also delegated this responsibility and kept the oven free for other cooking.

DEEP FRIED TURKEY

MAKES UP TO 14 SERVINGS DEPENDING ON THE WEIGHT OF THE BIRD

Directions:

Remove the giblets and neck from the turkey and reserve for other uses. Rinse turkey thoroughly with cold water and pat dry with paper towels. Drain the body cavity well. If the turkey has a plastic pop-up timer, remove it. Place the turkey in a large dish or roasting pan & rub the outside of turkey and the cavity with half of the seasoning mixture. Cover and refrigerate for 12 hours.

Drain the body cavity well and rub the turkey with the remaining seasoning and sprinkle some inside the body cavity.

Pour the peanut oil into a deep propane turkey fryer and heat to 325 degrees.

Place turkey on fryer rod. Wearing heavy-duty work gloves or an oven mitt and long sleeves, carefully lower the turkey into the hot oil with the rod attachment. Slowly increase the heat so the oil temperature returns to 325 to 350 degrees. Continued on next page...

Ingredients

1 – 14 pound turkey, fresh or frozen, thawed
1 8-ounce can of Cajun seasoning
4 gallons peanut oil

Set the turkey fryer up outside in an open area. Use a long-stemmed deep-fry thermometer that clips onto the rim of the turkey fryer to monitor the oil temperature.

Do not use a kitchen cook top for frying a whole turkey. The best and safest results come if you use a turkey fryer on an outdoor gas cooker with a propane tank.

One Thanksgiving when we got the turkey fryer out we discovered we had a hole in the pan.

This meant it would not hold the oil. We kept our humor as we rushed around looking for a back-up fryer. Fortunately a good neighbor had one he wasn't using. Whew!

DEEP FRIED TURKEY, continued

This may take some time. Fry the turkey approximately 45 minutes or 3 minutes per pound. Check for doneness with a meat thermometer inserted into the meaty part of the thigh. Temperature should register at least 180 degrees if turkey is done.

Remove turkey from oil, drain and let stand 20 to 30 minutes before slicing.

NOTES:

Always use peanut oil. It has a high smoke point and won't burn easily. If you're not sure how much to buy use these guidelines:

For a 10-12 pound bird use 2 ½ to 3 gallons of oil

For a 12 to 16 pound bird use 3 to 4 gallons of oil

When you lower the turkey into the hot oil, the oil may spatter. Wear a long sleeved shirt and work gloves.

Do not use the lid while frying and do not EVER leave the turkey and the cooker unattended.

Beef Prime Rib Roast Cooking Tips

A beef prime rib roast is an investment; therefore get the best one you can find. When selecting beef, look for meat that is bright red and well-marbled. Marbling—the distribution of white fat—is important to the flavor of the meat and also helps the leaner cuts, like prime rib, from drying out.

Remove the roast from the refrigerator at least 30 minutes prior to roasting to allow it to come close to room temperature.

To ensure ample servings plus leftovers, plan on approximately ½ to ¾ pound per person.

Carving a Prime Rib

A prime rib is not difficult to carve, provided you have a long, sharp slicing knife and a sturdy meat fork to steady the roast. Let the roast stand for 15 to 20 minutes after removing from the oven. This is so the roast can reabsorb its juices. This keeps it moist and tender and makes it easier to carve.

When ready to carve, place the roast, ribs down and fat side up, on a carving surface. Insert a carving fork into the top to steady it. Cut a ½ inch to ¾ inch vertical slice all the way down to the rib bone. Cut horizontally along the bone to free the slice.

Continue cutting parallel to the first slice, continuing to carve the slices as described for the first slice in the previous paragraph. As the bones are exposed, cut between them to remove them or leave them attached to a slice for guests who may prefer them. Cut only the number of slices required for the first serving.

Arrange the remaining uncut prime rib and the slices on a warm platter. Serve with the *au jus* sauce (or the natural juices from the roast)

For our Traditional Christmas Day Dinner

BEEF PRIME RIB ROAST WITH ROAST POTATOES

MAKES 6-8 SERVINGS

Ingredients

Prime rib roast with 3-4 bones, or 7-8 pounds trimmed weight.

2 Tablespoons chopped fresh thyme, or 1 teaspoon dried thyme.

Kosher salt

Freshly ground pepper

2-2 ½ pounds red potatoes, peeled and quartered.

Directions:

Position oven rack in the bottom third of oven and preheat oven to 475°

Place the roast, bottom side down on a roasting rack in a heavy roasting pan. Sprinkle with 1 Tablespoon of thyme and salt & pepper to taste; rub the spices in. Put roast into oven and after 5 minutes reduce the heat to 375° and continue roasting until the meat has reached the desired doneness. See the "Roasting Chart" on the following page. Start testing for doneness using an instant read thermometer after 1 ½ hours of roasting.

While the roast is cooking, put the potatoes in a large saucepan ¾ filled with water and bring them to a boil. Boil for 5 minutes, drain and set aside.

To achieve the desired degree of doneness, insert an instant-read thermometer into the center of the roast. Begin testing for doneness after about 1½ hours of cooking. While specific roasting times will vary depending on the size and shape of the roast, you can use the roasting chart below as a guide.

BEEF PRIME RIB ROAST WITH ROAST POTATOES, continued ...

After the meat has roasted 1 hour, arrange the potatoes in the pan around the roast. Turn the potatoes over in the pan juices to coat well, then sprinkle with the remaining 1 Tablespoon thyme, salt & pepper. Turn the potatoes over several times during the remaining roasting time to brown them evenly.

When the beef is toasted to the desired doneness, transfer it to a warmed platter. Cover loosely with aluminum foil and let sit 10-15 minutes before carving. If potatoes are not browned and tender, return them to the oven and continue to roast for an additional 5 to 10 minutes.

To make an *au jus* sauce, remove the fat from the juices in the pan by skimming it with a large spoon. Add ½ to 1 cup water to the pan and place over heat, stirring and scraping up any browned bits in the bottom of the pan. Boil this mixture for a few seconds. Taste for seasoning. To serve, place the *au jus* in a gravy boat and serve with the meat when sliced.

ROASTING CHART:

Internal Temperature & Roasting Time

Very Rare:

115°-12 min per pound

Rare:

120°-13min per pound

Medium Rare:

125°-14min per pound

Medium

135°-15 min per pound

Well-Done

145°-18 min per pound

This method is so easy and stress-free.

It is my preferred method – Can be served with Roasted or Mashed Potatoes.

EASY BEEF PRIME RIB ROAST

MAKES 6 – 8 SERVINGS

Ingredients

Prime rib roast with 3-4 bones, or 7-8 pounds trimmed weight.

2 Tablespoons Olive Oil

Coarse Ground Kosher or Sea Salt

Fresh Coarsely Ground Pepper

Directions:

Position oven rack in the bottom third of oven and preheat oven to 500°

Place the roast, bottom side down on a roasting rack in a heavy roasting pan. Coat the roast with olive oil, salt & pepper.

Place in 500° oven. After roasting for 10 minutes for each pound of roast, shut off the oven and let stand in the oven for two hours. Roast should be medium doneness. (Example: a 7 pound roast will roast at 500° for 70 minutes, then shut the oven off and let stand for 2 hours.)

To make an *au jus* sauce, remove the fat from the juices in the pan by skimming it with a large spoon. Add ½ to 1 cup water to the pan and place over heat, stirring and scraping up any browned bits in the bottom of the pan. Boil this mixture for a few seconds. Taste for seasoning. To serve, place the *au jus* in a gravy boat and serve with the meat when sliced.

This is part of our Traditional New Year's Day Dinner

Served with Mashed Potatoes, Black-eyed Peas & Collard Greens

SLOW COOKED PORK ROAST
with Sauerkraut

Ingredients

4-5 pounds Pork of your choice: Tenderloin, Pork Chops or Roast

1 Large Can or Package of Sauerkraut

Directions:

Place pork in a Crock Pot on Low. Pour Sauerkraut over top of pork and cook on Low for approximately 8 hours.

Serve with mashed potatoes, using the juice and kraut to flavor potatoes if desired.

On New Year's day this is the easiest meat dish ever and a family favorite.

My Family Recipes~

Serves:

Ingredients:

Directions:

My Family Recipes~

Serves:

Ingredients:

Directions:

My Family Recipes~

Serves:

Ingredients:

Directions:

My Family Recipes~

Serves:

Ingredients:

Directions:

My Family Recipes~

Serves:

Ingredients:

Directions:

Chapter 10

Vegetable Side Dishes

The secret to the creamiest mashed potatoes ever is using a ricer.

I didn't even know what a "ricer" was until my mother-in-law introduced me to this kitchen tool. Try Williams Sonoma or any cooking store with specialty items.

BASIC MASHED POTATOES

MAKES 24 SERVINGS

Ingredients

24 Medium mashed potatoes, peeled and cut into eighths (10-12 pounds)

18 Tablespoons butter, cut up

3 cups milk or half-and-half

1 ½ Tablespoons salt

1 ½ teaspoons pepper

Directions:

Put potatoes in a large pan and fill with enough water to cover. Bring to a boil for 15 minutes or until potatoes are tender. Drain well. Return potatoes to pan. Rice the potatoes with a ricer (available at cooking stores). Add butter, milk, salt and pepper and beat with an electric mixer until the desired consistency. Serve hot.

Notes:

Allow approximately ½ pound of raw potatoes per person.

Potatoes can be made a day in advance and reheated in the microwave oven.

This recipe is delicious.

I don't make it every year, but it is always a welcome alternate.

BUTTERBEANS WITH BACON

MAKES 6—8 SERVINGS

Ingredients

- 2 10-ounce packages frozen butterbeans
- 6 slices of bacon, cooked & crumbled, reserve the bacon drippings
- 4 green onions, chopped
- ½ cup fresh parsley, chopped
- ½ teaspoon coarse salt – sea salt or kosher salt
- ½ teaspoon freshly ground pepper

Directions:

Cook the butterbeans according to the package directions and set aside.

Sauté the green onions and garlic in the bacon drippings until tender. Stir in beans, parsley, salt & pepper. Cook just until heated through. Sprinkle with crumbled bacon.

This is a "Five Star" Family Favorite.

"It is the easiest and best side dish to serve with any meal."—Sabra Rice

CORN CASSAROLE

MAKES 8-10 SERVINGS

Ingredients

2 cans of corn

1 can cream of celery soup

1 sleeve buttery round crackers—crushed (I use Ritz Crackers)

¼ cup (1/2 stick) unsalted butter, melted

¼ cup chopped onions

1 cup (4 ounces) grated sharp cheddar cheese

Directions:

Preheat oven to 350°.

Spray inside of a 2 quart casserole with cooking spray.

Mix together corn, soup, onions and cheese. Pour mixture into casserole and bake for 20 minutes.

Combine cracker crumbs and melted butter. Sprinkle on top of casserole and return to oven for an additional 10 minutes.

Family Favorite and Classic Recipe

GREEN BEAN CASSEROLE

MAKES 6 SERVINGS

Ingredients

- 1 can cream of mushroom soup
- ½ cup 2% milk
- 1 teaspoon low sodium soy sauce
- 1/8 teaspoon freshly ground pepper
- 4 cups cooked green beans
- 1 1/3 cups canned French fried onions (I use French's)

Directions:

Preheat oven to 350° and spray a 1 ½ quart casserole with cooking spray.

Mix soup, milk, soy sauce, pepper, green beans & half of the fried onions together. Put the mixture into the casserole dish.

Bake for 25 minutes or until hot and bubbly.

Sprinkle remaining fried onions over top of the casserole and bake an additional 5 minutes or until onions are golden.

This is a Traditional Southern Recipe

It is an optional casserole occasionally served with the Traditional Turkey Dinner for guests who request it. Yellow Squash is primarily a summer squash and therefore not on all traditional Southern Fall and Winter holiday menus.

SOUTHERN SQUASH CASSEROLE

MAKES 6 SERVINGS

Ingredients

2 pounds yellow squash, sliced

1 cup of diced onions

2 Tablespoons butter, melted

1 ¼ cups round buttery cracker crumbs (18 crackers)

2 large eggs, beaten

1 ½ cups (6 ounces) shredded sharp cheddar cheese

¼ teaspoon coarse salt

¼ teaspoon freshly ground pepper

Directions:

Wash & cut squash. Cook in a small amount of water. Drain and mash; set aside.

Sauté onion in butter until tender.

Combine onion, squash, ¾ cups cracker crumbs, cheese, and remaining ingredients.

Spoon into a 2 quart casserole or an 11"x7" baking dish, which has been sprayed with vegetable cooking spray.

Sprinkle with remaining ½ cup cracker crumbs.

Bake uncovered at 350 degrees for 45 minutes.

Thanksgiving Menu Item.

In every crowd there will be a few who prefer sweet potatoes to traditional mashed potatoes. It's easy to make this ahead of time, and have it as an additional option on your Thanksgiving Table.

SWEET POTATO CASSEROLE

MAKES 8 SERVINGS

Directions:

Preheat the oven to 350°.

Poke holes in the sweet potatoes with a fork and arrange on a cookie sheet. Bake the sweet potatoes for 1 hour. Let cool, remove peels and mash in a large bowl. You should have approximately 3 2/3 cups of mashed sweet potato.

Combine mashed sweet potatoes with next 5 ingredients. Pour into an 11x7 inch baking dish that has been sprayed with cooking spray.

Sprinkle the topping mixture of brown sugar and chopped pecans over top of the potato mixture.

Bake for 35 minutes.

Ingredients

3 large sweet potatoes

½ cups packed brown sugar

2/3 cups chopped pecans

2 eggs

¼ cup orange juice

1 Tablespoon grated orange zest

1 teaspoon vanilla extract

1 teaspoon cinnamon

Dash of freshly grated nutmeg

Topping – ½ cup packed brown sugar and 1/3 cup chopped pecans

New Year's Day Menu

Tradition says to eat a lot of greens on New Year's Day

So you will attract money into your life for the coming year.

NEW YEAR'S POT OF GREENS
(For Prosperity)

MAKES 8 SERVINGS

Ingredients

3 pounds of fresh collard greens

2 medium red onions, finely chopped

2 Tablespoons olive oil

2 ½ cups vegetable broth

¼ cup apple cider vinegar

2 Tablespoons dark brown sugar

1 teaspoon kosher salt

½ teaspoon dried crushed red pepper

Directions:

Wash greens; trim and discard thick portions of the greens from leaves. Roll the leaves and cut in 1 inch pieces.

Sauté onions in hot oil in a Dutch oven over medium-high heat for 8 to 10 minutes or until tender. Add the vegetable broth, vinegar, brown sugar, salt and red pepper.

Gradually add collards to the pot and cook, stirring occasionally for 8 to 10 minutes or just until wilted. Reduce the heat to medium and continue to cook, stirring occasionally for 1 hour or until tender.

Simple and Delicious

ROASTED BRUSSEL SPROUTS

MAKES 8 SERVINGS

Directions:

Preheat oven to 400°.

Toss Brussel Sprouts with oil, salt and pepper in a baking pan and roast, stirring once or twice, until deep golden brown, crisp outside and tender inside, approximately 30 to 35 minutes. The outer leaves will be especially brown and crispy.

Transfer to a bowl and serve.

Ingredients

2 pounds Fresh Brussel Sprouts, trimmed and halved lengthwise

4 Tablespoons extra-virgin olive oil

1 teaspoon fine sea salt

1/2 teaspoon ground black pepper

My Family Recipes~

Serves:

Ingredients:

Directions:

My Family Recipes~

Serves:

Ingredients:

Directions:

My Family Recipes—

Serves:

Ingredients:

Directions:

My Family Recipes ~

Serves:

Ingredients:

Directions:

My Family Recipes ~

Serves:

Ingredients:

Directions:

Chapter 11

Turkey Leftovers & Miscellaneous

Family Favorite for any time of the year. This is a "Secret Sauce" recipe. Not sweet at all.

Makes a large batch to keep on hand any time you have pork or chicken.

Pour over shredded cabbage for Barbeque Slaw.

WAR EAGLE BARBEQUE SAUCE

MAKES 2 QUARTS

Ingredients

32 ounces ketchup

16 ounces mustard

16 ounces water

5 ½ ounces Worcestershire sauces

1 ½ ounce white vinegar

Dash of red pepper

Directions:

Mix ingredients together and store in a glass or plastic jar.

For an official A.U. Family Barbeque Sandwich … Hickory smoke a boneless Boston pork butt. Chip the meat and serve on a bun with A.U. Barbeque sauce. For slaw, mix cabbage and sauce. Serve with dill chips.

My youngest son has enjoyed boiling peanuts every year. When he was about 7 years old he started having his buddies to come over and share some peanuts from the pot. I caught him offering to sell bags of peanuts to the neighbors one year! Such a self-reliant and enterprising young man from an early age!

BOILED PEANUTS

Want another way to use your Turkey Fryer? We discovered this is a fun way to get the turkey fryer out early, check all the parts, get it cleaned up for Thanksgiving and have some fun, too! Every year around Halloween, just as the weather begins to change we make a 5 pound batch of boiled peanuts in the Turkey Fryer!

This is so easy! Boiled peanuts are a Southern favorite and generally you have to take a drive to the country to find someone who boils them in a large pot outdoors. They are best when they have been boiled overnight, and you can keep them for 2-3 days so long as you keep the pot simmering. Make certain if you do this it is outdoors in a safe & ventilated place where children and pets will not have unsupervised access.

You will need your Turkey Fryer, stand and propane gas. Wash 5 pounds of raw peanuts in the shells. Place the peanuts in the pot, cover with water and add 1 cup of coarse kosher salt. Bring the peanuts and water to a boil and let simmer for at least 3 hours. I like to start mine in the afternoon and in the evening I turn off the propane gas and let them sit overnight. In the morning I start the gas again and let them simmer on low.

Use a mesh strainer to dip out a scoop of peanuts when you are ready to eat them. Once the peanuts are boiled to the texture you desire, you can drain them and refrigerate them in the shells for up to a week. You can also store them for longer by placing them in quart sized zip lock bags and place them in the freezer

This dish can be made and frozen ahead of time using the chicken from the Homemade Chicken Broth you make several weeks before your event. Also a great thing to serve on the day you cooked the chicken broth.

Side dishes: Refrito Casserole & Spanish rice.

CHICKEN ENCHILADAS

MAKES 6—8 SERVINGS

Ingredients

- 4 Chicken Breasts
- 1 can green chicken enchilada sauce
- 1 small onion, diced
- 1 can cream of chicken soup
- 1 can chopped green chilies
- 1 clove garlic, minced
- 1 stick butter
- 1 small brick of Monterey Jack cheese with peppers
- 1 small brick Longhorn cheese
- 1 teaspoon dried oregano
- 1 ½ teaspoon ground cumin
- ¼ tsp cinnamon*
- ¼ to ½ teaspoon salt
- ¼ teaspoon pepper
- 12-16 corn tortillas

Directions:

Cook the chicken breasts (baked, boiled on top of range, or microwave). Dice cooked chicken & set aside. Grate cheeses and mix together, set aside.

Sauté' diced onions in a large fry pan with butter until soft, add garlic & green chilies. Mix well. Add diced chicken to the mixture. Add spices, and mix well. Let simmer about 15 to 20 minutes. After simmering, set the pan with the mixture aside.

Spray each corn tortilla with a little cooking spray and stack on a plate. Cover with paper towels and heat in the microwave 1-2 minutes until warm and soft. Spoon the chicken mixture into tortillas one at a time and roll them "jelly-roll" style. Place them seam side down in a 13"x9" pan sprayed with cooking spray.

Mix enchilada sauce & soup together and pour over rolled enchiladas, sprinkle cheeses on top.

Bake in a 350° oven for about 20-25 minutes. Serve with sour cream (or Greek yogurt), chopped tomatoes, and chopped lettuce.

Serve Refrito Casserole and Spanish rice with the Chicken Enchilada's (recipe on the previous page.) Any leftover Refrito Casserole can be heated to use as a dip with tortilla chips.

REFRITO CASSEROLE

MAKES A 4 CUP CASSAROLE

Ingredients

1 can traditional refried beans

1 can black beans

½ cup salsa

½ cup grated cheddar cheese

Directions:

Preheat Oven to 350°

Mix the ingredients together and place in a 1 quart casserole which has been sprayed with cooking spray. Bake with the chicken enchiladas, same temperature & time; 350° for 20-25 minutes.

5 minutes before you remove it from the oven, top with some additional cheddar cheese.

Great Recipe for Turkey Left-Overs!

TURKEY TETRAZZINI

MAKES 6—8 SERVINGS

Ingredients

1 pound linguine

1 ½ to 2 pounds leftover turkey, shredded or cut into chunks

½ pound breadcrumbs

½ cup mozzarella cheese, shredded

½ cup parmesan cheese, grated

2 cups or more to taste – Alfredo sauce (recipe to follow)

Coarse salt & freshly ground pepper to taste

Directions:

Cook pasta approximately 5-7 minutes until al dente. Drain pasta and mix with remaining ingredients. Pour into a baking dish which has been sprayed with vegetable cooking spray. Top with additional mozzarella cheese and bake covered in a 350 degree oven for 20 minutes. Uncover and bake an additional 5 minutes.

Casserole should be golden and bubbly.

For variations you can use chicken &/or add vegetables such as English peas or broccoli. This dish is so easy and everyone loves it! It freezes well, too.

Use for Turkey Tetrazzini

This Recipe makes enough to keep on hand for several recipes.

ALFREDO SAUCE

MAKES 1 ¾ QUARTS OF SAUCE

Ingredients

1 cup grated parmesan cheese

1 Tablespoon salt

½ cup unsalted butter

2 quarts heavy cream

1 Tablespoon white pepper

1 ½ teaspoon dried oregano

1 ½ teaspoon dried basil

1 Tablespoon cornstarch

Directions:

Add all ingredients except the cornstarch to a medium saucepan and cook over medium-high heat until it comes to a boil. Add cornstarch & stir well.

Remove from heat & stir occasionally until thick.

Sauce will continue to thicken until it cools. Store in glass mason jars or plastic freezer containers until ready to use.

This recipe makes enough for several casseroles.

Delicious Turkey Sandwich for Turkey Leftovers!

Family Favorite

HOT BROWN SANDWICHES

MAKES 6—8 SERVINGS

Ingredients

Cheese Sauce:
2 Tablespoons unsalted butter
¼ cup all-purpose flour
2 cups milk
¼ cup shredded sharp Cheddar cheese
¼ cup grated Parmesan cheese
¼ teaspoon salt
½ teaspoon Worcestershire Sauce

Sandwiches:
8 Slices trimmed toast (French or Italian bread is really good)
1 pound sliced turkey breast
8 slices tomato
8 slices bacon, partially cooked
4 ounces grated Parmesan cheese

Directions:

Cheese Sauce:

Melt butter in saucepan; blend in flour. Add milk, cheeses and seasonings, stirring constantly until smooth and thickened. Set Aside.

Sandwiches:

Preheat oven to 400°.

Cut toast into triangles and put in a baking dish. Arrange turkey slices on toast and cover with hot cheese sauce; top with tomato and bacon. Sprinkle with Parmesan cheese and bake at 400° until bubbly.

My Family Recipes~

Serves:

Ingredients:

Directions:

My Family Recipes ~

Serves:

Ingredients:

Directions:

My Family Recipes ~

Serves:

Ingredients:

Directions:

My Family Recipes ~

Serves:

Ingredients:

Directions:

My Family Recipes~

Serves:

Ingredients:

Directions:

My Family Recipes ~

Serves:

Ingredients:

Directions:

Appendix A

Who's Coming This Year

Who's Coming This Year

Who's Coming This Year

Appendix B

Holiday Preparation List & Time Table

3-6 Weeks Ahead:

- ☐ Make your guest list. Call, write or email to confirm who is coming, when they will arrive and their departure times.
- ☐ Confirm with anyone bringing items – in our family it is my sister-in-law who always brings the breadcrumbs for the dressing – and confirm how much will be needed.
- ☐ Make plans for guests sleeping arrangements
- ☐ Check supply of tables, chairs, dishes, glasses, utensils and linens
- ☐ Prepare your menus and gather any recipes needed
- ☐ Clean out your pantry and freezer; you'll need the space
- ☐ Order the Honey Baked Ham
- ☐ Shop for non-perishable groceries and the perishable items you will need for make ahead recipes
- ☐ Make chicken broth (x2) and freeze half; reserve the other half for the Turkey Gravy
- ☐ Make Turkey Gravy and freeze (x2)
- ☐ Make pie crusts (x8); double wrap in plastic wrap and freeze
- ☐ Cook pumpkin (unless you want to use canned) and freeze in 1.5 or 3 cup containers.

- ☐ Some cakes &/or cookie dough can be made ahead and frozen
- ☐ Squash for casserole can be cooked and frozen at this time

Holiday Preparation List & Time Table, continued ...

1-2 Weeks Ahead:

- ☐ Get out dishes, silver, glasses & wash or polish as needed, iron table linens, if needed
- ☐ Stock up on extra soap, paper towels, dish washing soaps, napkins, toilet paper, paper and plastic utensils, etc.
- ☐ Make a large batch of chocolate fudge candy
- ☐ Shop for any remaining non-perishable items you will need

One Week Ahead:

- ☐ Make cranberry sauce
- ☐ Make pinwheels, roll & refrigerate in plastic wrap
- ☐ Make cookies & candies
- ☐ Clean the house
- ☐ Purchase THE Turkey (or Roast) ... a fresh Turkey from Whole Foods can be stored in the refrigerator for up to 10 days.

Three days before your first guests arrive:

- ☐ Finish up cookie baking
- ☐ Move pie crusts from freezer to refrigerator to thaw

Two days before your first guests arrive:

- ☐ Shop for perishables
- ☐ Clean the bathrooms
- ☐ Tidy house for final cleaning
- ☐ Move chicken broth, gravy, pumpkin & squash to refrigerator for thawing

That day your first guests arrive:

- ☐ Pick up the Honey Baked Ham
- ☐ Start cooking pies
- ☐ Change the linens on the beds
- ☐ Vacuum
- ☐ Set goodies out on the dessert table
- ☐ Wait for the arrival of guests

The day before your big dinner:

- ☐ Bake any remaining pies, usually custard &/or pumpkin
- ☐ Make the mashed potatoes
- ☐ But a big pot of 15 bean soup or chili on the stove for dinner
- ☐ Have someone help get the tables in place so they can be set early in the morning

Feast Day:

- ☐ Omelet Casserole for Breakfast so everyone can help themselves
- ☐ Set the tables
- ☐ Prepare the turkey to go in the oven no later than 11:00 a.m. (if roasting)
- ☐ Put out crudities, appetizers and punch to be munched on throughout the day
- ☐ Put together casseroles in time to be cooked as soon as the turkey is out of the oven
- ☐ Make The Dressing
- ☐ Put out the cranberry sauce and butter
- ☐ Put together breakfast casserole after dinner & refrigerate so it will be ready for to pop in the oven early the next morning.

Appendix C

Meal Schedule

Day/Date: _____

Dinner Guests ( ) - Main Course: _____

Day/Date: _____

Breakfast ( ) – Continental

Lunch ( ) – Catch as Catch Can – Good Luck!

Dinner ( ) - _____

Day/Date: _____

Breakfast ( ) – Breakfast Buffet

Lunch ( ) - _____

Dinner ( ) - _____

Day/Date: _____

Breakfast ( ) – Jay's Omelet Casserole

Lunch: snack all day – Soup, Ham & Cheese, appetizers and crudities

Dinner ( ) THE Turkey Dinner!

Day/Date: _____

Breakfast ( ) – Breakfast Buffet

Lunch & Beyond – Help eat leftovers!

Arrivals:

Day/Date: _____

Day/Date: _____

Day/Date: _____

Day/Date: _____

Appendix D

Pre-Holiday Shopping List

(Nonperishable & make ahead recipe items)

MEAT:

- ☐ 1 whole chicken fryer (for chicken broth)
- ☐ Turkey pieces (to make turkey broth for gravy)

BAKING:

- ☐ 15# all-purpose flour
- ☐ 1# bag M&M chocolate candies
- ☐ 15# granulated sugar
- ☐ 2# brown sugar
- ☐ 8# confectioner's sugar
- ☐ 1 can evaporated milk
- ☐ 1 can condensed milk
- ☐ 16 ounces (2 boxes) unsweetened chocolate
- ☐ 1 box cocoa powder
- ☐ White corn syrup (1 cup)
- ☐ 1 bottle (1 ounce) red food coloring (if making red velvet cake)
- ☐ Vanilla extract
- ☐ Almond extract
- ☐ Baking powder
- ☐ Baking soda
- ☐ Tapioca, quick cooking

- ☐ Poultry seasoning
- ☐ Pumpkin pie spice OR cinnamon & nutmeg
- ☐ Ground pepper, freshly ground
- ☐ Kosher salt
- ☐ Instant coffee granules, small

Appendix E

Thanksgiving Holiday Shopping List

Last Trip to the Store – Perishables

- ☐ Turkey – fresh, never been frozen
- ☐ Celery – 2 bunches
- ☐ Onions, 3#
- ☐ Purple Onions – 1
- ☐ Parsnip
- ☐ Celriac (if you can find it – used for cooking roasted turkey)
- ☐ Turnip
- ☐ Fresh poultry herbs & poultry seasoning
- ☐ Yellow squash, 1.5# (if not previously cooked & frozen)
- ☐ Bell peppers — 2
- ☐ Coffee, freshly ground—2 pounds
- ☐ Cheese, sliced for ham sandwiches
- ☐ Bread for sandwiches
- ☐ Eggs – 4 to 5 dozen
- ☐ Milk
- ☐ Half & half
- ☐ Cream
- ☐ Coffee creamer (optional – can use half & half)
- ☐ Whipped cream
- ☐ Orange juice

- ☐ Organic mixed greens
- ☐ Caesar salad dressing, 1 pint
- ☐ Guacamole dip, fresh made if available
- ☐ Tortilla chips for guacamole
- ☐ Potatoes

Appendix F

Memories & Traditions ...

Here are some of our memories & traditions ... you can start a page of your own and add it to YOUR planning guide!

1990 was my first of these Thanksgiving Reunions in Georgia. It was Mima who had instilled the importance of these gatherings in us all. Attendance was mandatory – unless you lived so far away that you just could not get here. This was the first holiday in many years that she had all of her three children and their families with her.

Pie baking was of great importance to Mima, especially pumpkin & custard pies. The last two years she came to our reunions she transported no less than 12 pies to the event. We ate pies, gave them away, sent them home with folks, and still had pies left over. Mima had two requirements of me as her new daughter-in-law. First, I had to give her baby boy a son, second that I learn to make a good pie crust. Thankfully, I was able to do both.

1991 was Mima's last Holiday Reunion. I had produced the grandson for her baby boy. She brought her pies, and her husband brought videos of football games in stood in front of the TV watching re-plays. Her health was failing and this was her last reunion. Our next reunion was the following June for her funeral. We all were there and realized how IMPORTANT it is for us all to gather together each year and how much fun we all have together. The Annual Thanksgiving Reunion Tradition was set in stone!

By 1993 our Thanksgiving Reunions had become a "Tradition" and I began recording them … That year I wrote:

"We had a marvelous Thanksgiving this year. There were 16 who sat down to dinner on Thanksgiving Day. The whole week was filled with festivity, family and food, food, food. The first guests arrived on Monday and the rest of the crew arrived Wednesday evening."

Granddad Turned 70 this year on Tuesday of the week … We celebrated by honoring him with a special birthday cake & he told a hilarious story about his remote control golf caddy going into a lake and he had to follow it right into the lake to retrieve it.

Our 2 Year Old son woke the entire house on Tuesday morning when his dad tried to carry him downstairs to me. He screamed at his Dad, so loudly that it woke the entire house, "Daddy, you are NOT MY FRIEND!" Started everyone's morning off with a good laugh!

When my daughter was only four years old she began anticipating the Event a month in advance … As soon as she saw that I'd begun the baking and freezing she began getting ready by "practicing" sleeping in her sleeping bag before the guests arrived. She knew she'd be giving up her bedroom for someone!

The kids played "Sneak-A-Snack" even though no one cared they were eating the goodies. It took several years for all the adults to figure out that they had invented RULES for this game!

Two of our nephews had a Pumpkin Pie Eating Contest. They each had to eat ½ of a pumpkin pie with whipped cream. The one to finish his pie and whistle first won. The victor won with a time of 3 minutes and 38 seconds!

My sister-in-law made delicious Bread Dressing which she mixed in a 5 Gallon paint bucket! She mashed the potatoes with a ricer (you can purchase one of these at Williams & Sonoma) and then whipped them using my husband's drill & paint mixer. I later bought a large commercial stainless bowl to use at these events. HOWEVER, please notice – you can always think outside the box and improvise when necessary!

Both the men and the boys played their usual pranks on one another. One of the teenage nephews was initiated into the games with a glass of cold water in the shower and spaghetti noodles in his sleeping bag. Nephew retaliated appropriately.

Annual Holiday Reunion Weigh In! I only know of one female in our group who EVER had the nerve to participate in this game. Just prior to dinner the men and boys who wanted to participate would weigh in on the scales. The number was recorded and after dinner they weighed again. The one who had gained the most weight won! Somehow this never really excited me, but I enjoyed watching those boys have fun with it. There wasn't any particular prized other than the "winning" of the challenge. Yep, I'd say that is reflective and true. They were happy "winning" just for the sake of "winning" the competition. One nephew even had "strategy" for this. He plans what he eats from the day before and through the meal! Personally, my goal was generally to try NOT to gain weight during the event!

The year when the Turkey Fryer to start it up on the big day—there was a HOLE in it! Oh no! However the potential disaster turned into a comical scavenger hunt as my husband scoured the neighborhood for someone to loan him a pot! Someone who wasn't using their own turkey fyer! Mission accomplished! Remember it is not the crisis, but how it is handled that makes or breaks the event! Count on the unpredictable and the unexpected to happen – with a gathering of this many it is the one thing you can count on!

Uncle Jay's Omelets ... For years Uncle Jay would cook each person an omelet, made- to- order on Thanksgiving morning. Quite an undertaking when there are more than 20 people in the house! This turned into a very popular tradition, and we had "rules": You had to put your own name on a list to get your omelet. No one else could put your name on the list for you. This meant you had to wake up early if you didn't want to wait until brunch time for it; he always cooked in the order of the list. The list wasn't started until Thanksgiving Morning. This prevented anyone from starting the list the night before, and made sure everyone on the list was up to get their omelet! Uncle Jay passed away ... but we all think of him especially at Thanksgiving. Everyone loved him so much and he is sorely missed. He always made special time for our last minute runs to the grocery store, was available in the kitchen for short order requests, and always took the kids out to do something fun during the weekend. Oh yeah, and he always made sure the host and hostess were also entertained. He and my sister and law always showed up first and took us out to a delightful dinner and he always ordered the best wine. Although his made-to-order omelets are irreplaceable, we now serve omelet casserole, which we have named after him, on Thanksgiving morning.

We all have a wonderful time each year anticipating, preparing for, and hosting the Annual Holiday Reunion. I love having family here and feel fortunate to be a part of a family that has so much fun when they are together ... which reminds me ... Please, please, always remember to count your blessings and be thankful for this time together and for each other. Focus on the fun and the family!

Appendix G

Thanksgiving or Holiday Games

Our Holiday Feast is loads of fun and we have a few traditions and games to share. I'm sure you can come up with some of your own but here are a few that we do each year.

Thanksgiving Feast Weigh In

This one is not for those who are sensitive about their weight. I can only remember one of the women who ever participated in this contest, and although I'm not recommending this to those of you who are watching their figure, I will tell you that quite frequently it was one of our healthiest nephews with the best physique who would win this contest.

Prior to the "Big Feast" everyone weighs in. After the "Big Feast" they weigh in again. The person who gained the most weight during the Thanksgiving Feast wins. I'm not giving away any hints about the winning strategies … but there are some!

Pie Eating Contest

This is a timed contest so you will need a clock with a minute hand or a stop watch, and a pumpkin pie topped with whipped cream and a willing referee. It was started by two of our nephews who both loved my homemade pumpkin pie. Divide the pie into two equal parts. On the count of go … the timer starts and each person eats half a pie – the first one to finish his pie and whistle is the winner. Record the time for future events so you can have a record breaking winner! Winning time is currently 3 minutes & 38 seconds!

Sneak-A-Snack

This game was created by the children, who didn't know that the grownups had already decided that during this week we were not going to fret over what, how much or when they ate. We always have a big dessert table out and lots of food choices. The kids thought they were sneaking food, and they began calling this game Sneak-A-Snack. It took us adults years to figure out they even had rules, and here they are:

1. You have to be a kid to play Sneak-A-Snack.
2. You have to Sneak-A-Snack from the dessert table without being seen by a grownup.
3. If a grown up sees you sneaking the snack then you are "dead", which means you are frozen and cannot move until another kid touches you.
4. If that kids gets seen then he is dead too.

NOTE: You better hope you don't run out of kids.

Pranks:

Rule #1 – be ready to play when you arrive!

Rule #2 – After you play ONE prank on someone then you are in the game for all time, year after year.

Rule #3 – If you don't want to be pranked, then don't EVER prank anyone!

Rule #4 – No fair playing pranks that make real big messes that the hostess has to clean up!

Rule #5 – This is all for fun – one ever gets hurt in any way!

A prank to get you started … spaghetti noodles (cooked) in the bottom of the bed or sleeping bag. Rice (uncooked) in a bed or sleeping bag works, too!

Most ingenious prank – 5 Gal bucket of water, rigged to dump on my husband's head when he walked into his shop.

Have FUN! That is the spirit of the celebration and the fun of the family all getting together!

Following you will find a few additional pages in which you can record your own memories and traditions from your holiday gatherings.

Family Memories & Traditions

Family Memories & Traditions

Family Memories & Traditions

Family Memories & Traditions

Family Memories & Traditions